LIFE CHOICES

LIFE
CHOICES

How to Make the Critical Decisions
—About Your
Education, Career, Marriage,
Family, Life Style

Gordon Porter Miller

THOMAS Y. CROWELL, Publishers

Established 1834   New York

FIRST EDITION

Designed by C. Linda Dingler

Library of Congress Cataloging in Publication Data

Miller, Gordon Porter.
    Life choices.

    1. Decision-making.   I. Title.
BF441.M54   1978   158'.1   78-3860
ISBN 0-690-01721-9

78 79 80 81 82 10 9 8 7 6 5 4 3 2 1

To my wife Heide—

*a good decision with so many
beautiful outcomes*

Contents

Acknowledgments

Decision-making theory is familiar to many business-school graduates, economic planners, and mathematicians. But it has been neglected as a tool for dealing with personal choices because it has rarely been translated into a form that people can easily understand and apply to everyday life. In order to make this tool practical, I have pulled together from many sources a variety of theories, experiences, and observations relating to the decision-making process.

Many people have been especially helpful to me in this work. Dr. H. B. Gelatt—who was the first person to write about the widely practical applications of decision-making, and has never received enough recognition for his fresh and viable ideas—has generously shared his thoughts with me. Dr. Charles Morris, my doctoral adviser at Columbia, first encouraged me in my work on decision-making and was always available when it came to giving his precious time to help others clarify their ideas. The College Entrance Examination Board provided me with an arena for experimentation, capped by a sabbatical leave during which most of the writing was done.

Many thanks are due also to decision-making consultants across the country who challenged and shared ideas on my new approaches; to my students and clients in schools, colleges, prisons, and adult-education programs who shared their critical choices with me; to my children—Kenneth, Sabina, Ingrid, and Thomas—who gave up their time with their dad so that deadlines could be met; and finally, to that small group of counselors, teachers, managers, and others who have spent their time and energies trying out these concepts with their clients.

It is my hope that this book will be a small payment to all these people who have helped me sustain the belief that informed decision-making is essential to effective living and learning.

Foreword

This time like all times is a very good one
if we but know what to do with it.
—Ralph Waldo Emerson

When people at a party ask me "What do you do for a living," I say that I write materials and train people to learn how to make decisions. A long conversation inevitably follows, usually starting with how much frustration, difficulty, and sheer agony they associate with the act of choosing, and then moving to the specific decision situations that they have faced or are anticipating. The problems they describe range from the small nagging choices involved in planning a social event or vacation to crucial dilemmas about education, job satisfaction, career change, personal relationships, their children's futures, and overall life style.

The intensity of their interest and concern never surprises me. Life is full of choices, and regardless of age, background, or personal circumstances, people find it difficult to make decisions. The sad fact of the matter is that little has been done in schools, colleges, families, and business settings to equip us to make choices wisely. We may go to college, get married, raise a family, follow a career, relocate, and retire—all critical, or life-shaping, decision opportunities—without ever actually making a well-considered, well-informed choice. The main reason for this is obvious: we have not learned to go about deciding in a rational, effective way. Consequently, few of us have a hand in consciously determining our lives.

The tragic results of poor decision-making became

apparent to me more than ten years ago when, as a member of the College Entrance Examination Board's Guidance Division, I began to study the way young people were using information to make decisions relating to education, career plans, and the use of leisure time. In general, I found that regardless of the quality of their information, they tended to go along with societal expectations or with what had been done before by others like them. Rarely did they make choices based on what was important to them. Frequently, very frequently, they actually let others make decisions for them. Good information might have been helpful, but it was clearly not enough to insure reaching a good decision. What these individuals lacked was a *process for deciding*, some way of integrating available information with their *personal needs and priorities.*

These findings, and a thorough review of existing research about personal decision-making, pointed to the need for materials and training activities to teach the skills involved in making a good decision. In 1971, the College Board established its new, nationwide Decision-Making Program under my direction. The initial purpose of this program was to develop decision-making materials for youngsters in grades 7–9. The effort was so well received and the need so widespread that additional program components were subsequently developed for all age levels, from kindergarten through all stages of adulthood. As a trained counselor, I was able to observe firsthand how dissatisfied people were with their lives, and how so much of this dissatisfaction stemmed from their inability to make effective choices for themselves. Now, over seven years later, decision-making concepts have become integrated into school and college curriculums, as well as in noneducational settings such as businesses and social agencies, and in human-resources and career-development programs.

The need and interest continue to escalate, and during the past three years alone, I have conducted more than three hundred training sessions in decision-making for people from all walks of life, in most states and in several foreign countries.

Why this widespread interest in learning to decide? There are many reasons, but most come down to the fact that people simply do not like what life is showing them. In our technologically advanced and rapidly changing society, as individuals operate in the context of uncertainty, they are realizing more than ever the need to gain control of their lives and to combat the sense of powerlessness that seems to move them further away from getting what they want.

The seminars and training sessions I have conducted over the past few years have touched thousands of individuals: teenagers struggling to discover their goals and identity, adults trying to deal with pressing personal and career problems, retired persons wanting to make the most of the rest of their lives, prisoners trying to build for the future even as they suffer the consequences of tragic choices in the past. The fact is that decision-making relates to everybody. No one's freedom is so unlimited or life so hopeless that he cannot benefit from learning decision-making skills.

Even in the course of short seminars, I have observed the impact of the decision-making process on people's lives. Hopelessness has changed to hope, confusion has been replaced by direction, the feeling of powerlessness has been followed by a quest for control, and fears of doing have given way to positive action.

This book distills the content and process of these seminars and training sessions into a practical, usable decision-making model that can be applied to any type of choice relating to personal, career, or educational matters. The cases are all drawn directly from life. The exercises and procedures have been tried by people of all ages and in all kinds of critical decision situations. They provide a valuable and indispensable tool for living a more effective and satisfying life.

LIFE CHOICES

1.

Life Is Choice

It's much easier to ride a horse in the direction he's going.

—Werner Erhard

How do you feel about yourself? Is your life satisfying? Are you growing emotionally and intellectually?

Are you satisfied with where you live? With your job? Your income?

Would you like to alter your relationships with some of the people in your life?

Are you happy with the way you spend your leisure time? Did you enjoy your last vacation?

Have you been faced with any decisions lately? Did you benefit from the choice you made?

All of these questions have something to do with decisions you have made—or have let others make for you. You are probably satisfied with some and dissatisfied with others.

Throughout life, we are faced with countless decisions. Once acted upon, they shape our lives. If we learn to make decisions skillfully, thus using our resources to best advantage, we can narrow the gap between what we want and what appears to be possible. Unfortunately, many of us don't and suffer the consequences.

Each year thousands of teenagers go to college only because it is expected of them. Untold numbers of men and women marry and raise families without actually deciding to do so at all. Others struggle along for a lifetime in unsatisfying occupations. These people are victims of not knowing how to make decisions. Frequently, they are not even aware of alternative choices. As a result, they deny themselves the lives they would like to live if they only knew how.

Yet other people do manage to get what they want. Consider the woman successfully pursuing a career in business while continuing to raise a happy family; the young executive who leaves a prestigious position to do something far less lucrative that makes his life much happier; and the retiree who begins to study law at fifty-two and becomes a successful practicing lawyer. Do these people owe their success to luck, innate ability, unusual financial resources, no family responsibilities? Not at all! They simply learned how to decide—to establish what they want and move toward it in a rational, systematic way. They learned to manage their lives by making well-considered choices. You, too, can learn how to use what you know to get what you want.

Throughout your life, you have constantly been asked to make up your mind. By now, you should have developed some real skills as a decision-maker. And as with any skill that improves with practice, you should more and more enjoy the prospect of making choices. After all, you've probably had more chances to utilize this skill than any other. Why, then, do people tend to feel so frustrated when they face important decisions?

The fact is that most people have developed no rational or coherent method for dealing with their many opportunities to take action. And despite the importance of decision-making, the opportunity seldom arises in our educational settings, in our jobs, or even in our family relationships for us to learn how to decide. Indeed, it can be argued that these institutions often do their best to discourage decision-making on the part of individuals. It is almost as though they are afraid to equip people with the information they need to decide for themselves. It is not difficult to understand why. The institutions we look to for direction—government, universities, and even the family—are slow to respond to change. Often, in fact, they do their best to deny the existence of change. Major problems facing all of us—energy conservation, equality, unemployment, urban decay, family relations—are simply not being addressed by our institutions in any clear, definitive way. And this further compounds our anxieties and difficulties when it comes to deciding as individuals. Consequently, while you are expected to make up your mind, you may not know how to go about it.

Recently, in one of my training seminars, I asked the group members what they thought about or felt when faced with a decision. Most of their responses stressed the anxiety involved. They felt decision-making was complex, painful, risky, and tiring. They worried about lacking information, acting before feeling confident, giving up the known for the unknown, making mistakes. They were concerned about the time and social pressures involved, and about how their decisions affected other people important in their lives. In short, for the majority, decision-making was a chore imposed by a crisis—not an opportunity to shape and control their lives, or to move toward more freedom of action.

"If I can handle me, I can handle it all"

While it is easy to get caught in a life of little choice, it is possible to steer your life toward the goals you desire. The process begins with you, the individual decider. The quote above is from an inmate in a maximum-security prison; it is the starting point for most of us. You have to *want* to decide. The sense of powerlessness that you may feel at this point in your life is something that will begin to disappear as you apply the decision-making skills that you will find in this book.

Note the use of the word "skills." This term is rarely paired with "decision-making" in daily conversation. More often, someone is described as being "decisive" or as having "a talent for making decisions." Such remarks imply that the ability to make decisions is innate, that a fortunate few people may be born with it, but the rest of us just have to accept being wishy-washy as our lot in life.

Actually, the opposite is true. Good decision-making requires the exercise of learned skills. To some extent, you learn these skills from your experiences as you grow up; but all too frequently our knowledge of them remains incomplete through adulthood. Like all others, however, these skills can be learned through conscious effort.

Particularly when facing an important, critical decision, the person lacking decision-making skills is inclined to feel inadequate and frightened by the prospect of having to choose. Finally, he or she is likely to back off, figuring that no outcome at all is better than a bad outcome. But of course there is always an outcome regardless of what, or whether, you decide.

Thus if you put off deciding whether to quit the job you hate, you are, in effect, choosing to keep the job. If you say you can't decide about that trip to Europe, the outcome is the same as if you had decided not to go. If you avoid deciding whether you need a change of life style, the end is the same as if you decided to stay with your old way of life.

By not deciding, you forfeit the opportunity to achieve a better or different outcome. Even if you stay with your existing situation, it should be a conscious choice among various alternatives—not merely what was left when you couldn't make up your mind. And remember that even the "leftover" course could have outcomes that you may have failed to consider.

The skills you acquire in this book can be applied to virtually all the important decisions that you will face in your life. Making these decisions is not a simple process. Some uncertainty will usually exist. But you can advance at your own pace, and you should practice all the time. From the beginning, each decision will be a kind of approximation of what you want. No single decision is an absolute answer, but with each choice you will be steadily advancing toward your goals.

Ultimately, learning a decision-making process and applying it means translating what you say you want into action. It is taking a close look at yourself and those around you. It is learning to think for yourself. It is discovering what is really important to you and just how important. It is learning to use your freedom to direct your own life. It is taking action. And, finally, it is learning to be responsible for the actions you take. In short, it is using the knowledge of who you are and what you want to be in a rational process that will move you toward attaining the goals you want in life. For if you don't *know* what you want, you'll probably never get it.

Freedom Is a Risky Business

One of the main reasons for learning how to make decisions is to increase your personal freedom, to add to your available options. But it isn't all that easy. A proliferation of choices accompanies our free society: the freedom to improve yourself, to pursue the profession of your choice, to speak openly, and to expect equal opportunity and treatment. While these freedoms exist, they may be of little value to you unless you can use them.

A young man serving a long prison term said to me: "Freedom is a risky business; you can choose to go to hell in so many different ways." He was reflecting on his own life and how his freedom to choose had led him to a long sentence behind bars.

Yes, freedom is a risky business—for all of us. In fact, it can be downright terrifying. Consider the multitude of choices available to you in virtually all facets of life. You can take part in any number of close personal relationships, when not long ago marriage would have been the only acceptable option. You can get college credit for experience, when formerly you could get it only by attending class. You can change careers in mid-life, when once you were locked into a business or profession. If you are a woman, you can now choose to work when you have small children; and if you are a man, you may even choose to quit your job to stay home with the kids!

Nonetheless, it often appears that the more possibilities you have, the more impossible it is to choose. Many of the people I work with who have difficulty making decisions get angry with me because I constantly encourage them to develop and consider as many options as possible in a given situation. Exasperated, they say it was easier when they only knew a few possibilities. Some of them beg me to make the decision for them. It is true that having more options makes choosing more difficult. But it is also true that more options give you greater freedom and a far better chance to move toward the life plan that is most satisfying to you.

To get the feeling of what is involved when you have a lot of alternatives from which to choose, think about some of the things that you'd really like to do. Then select one thing above all others that you'd like to be paid for doing. Write it down.

While this may appear to be a relatively easy choice to make, many of us really struggle with it. Why? Because there are so many things we like to do that it's difficult to select one above all others. What if you leave out the most important thing of all? Are there things you're not even aware of that you might put down if only you knew about them?

In short, when it comes to choosing something from a large number of even "pleasant" alternatives, the choice can be difficult. It's not unlike walking into an ice-cream store that offers thirty different flavors. Some of these are familiar, others sound appealing, and still others are totally unknown. Where once we could have expected to find only vanilla, chocolate, and strawberry, we are now confronted with such flavors as rocky road, banana, shortbread, and chocolate divine. The possibilities are fantastic. How can anyone decide? It is not difficult to envision the unskilled decision-maker, asked to make up his mind, stammering out, "Vanilla," when one of the other flavors would have been much more satisfying.

And so it is when you face the prospect of alternatives in a more critical decision situation. In scrambling for a way to a meaningful life, we find paradoxically an abundance of choices marked by an increased sense of the loss of freedom.

Preventing the Loss of Freedom

Pause a moment to think about what you want in life. If you have trouble deciding, don't worry. Many of us haven't taken the time to think beyond the present. You may have to dream a little or fantasize. Think about anything you want, even if it seems impossible. Consider the life style you'd like in the future, the kinds of things you'd like to be doing, the people you'd like to be with, the satisfactions you'd like to experience. Write down the things that you really want. Think of the things you want as a kind of ceiling on your life. Make sure it's your ceiling and not the one somebody has prescribed for you. Remember, you're absolutely free to decide anything you want at this point.

Material things I want to own:
People I want to be with:
Satisfactions I want to feel:
Things I want to achieve in work:
Things I want to achieve in personal growth:
Things I want to achieve in leisure pursuits:

Examine your choices carefully. Are your listings complete? Can you expand the number of choices in each category? Now imagine that this exercise is suddenly a real-life decision situation for you. Would you like more time to add to your choices?

As you expand your freedom of choice by developing more possibilities for action, you are taking the first steps toward bringing about greater control over what you want your life to be. An abundance of choices may be initially confusing, but the value of having a large number of possibilities to work with far outweighs any disadvantages.

A decision can be developed through a kind of decisions tree, which is often used to demonstrate the major ingredients in the decision-making process. The usefulness of the "tree" is that it can show the increasingly complex number of "branches," or opportunities, that arise from a single decision. A variation of this procedure can help you focus on the element of freedom in your past choices. Each decision you have made to date has some implications for your future. Some have been helpful in getting you closer to what you want. Others have probably diverted you. Beginning with the bottom of the tree, identify one important decision at some stage in your life and describe how it helped or hindered your progress toward what you want—at the top of the tree. For example, if you chose a certain major in college or opted not to get married, how did these choices give direction to—or divert you from—what you want in life in terms of a career, personal relationships, overall satisfaction?

YOUR FREEDOM IN DECISIONS TREE

How freedom and opportunities led to what you want in life. Satisfactions gained or anticipated.

_____

_____

_____

Things that you didn't want to happen. Satisfaction lost or forfeited.

_____

_____

_____

How freedom and opportunities led to things unexpected but important to you. Satisfactions gained or anticipated.

Unanticipated freedom and opportunities gained.

_____

_____

_____

_____

_____

Freedoms and opportunities lost permanently or temporarily.

Expected freedom and opportunity gained.

_____

_____

_____

A Critical Life Choice

_____

_____

You should begin to see how your decisions shape your life and even represent what you are. Observe how each decision has some impact on subsequent opportunities. Like all of us, you have had to deal with the element of freedom along the way. Did you really freely decide what was important to you?

While you are developing your skills as a decider, you will become increasingly aware of situations in which your freedom to decide is being violated. You will also see that loss of control in your life is in fact less often the result of a lack of legal or personal freedom than it is of a lack of knowledge and experience in knowing how to go about making a choice. You will increasingly find the need to take active control over shaping your life. The purpose of this book is to give you the decision-making tools that can make your life choices count for you—and lead toward ever greater freedom, opportunity, and satisfaction.

2.
Little Decisions, Big Decisions

I never realized how many decisions I have
had in my lifetime and how few of them I
have made myself.
—Participant in decision-making seminar

What, then, is a decision? In its simplest form, a decision
is a choice between two or more courses of action, ideally
made after a comparison of other possible actions and
their possible consequences. *For a decision to be made,
there must be more than one possibility to choose from.*
If your problem is what to eat tonight, a restaurant menu
with more than one offering will provide an opportunity
for you to decide. On the other hand, if you sit down to
dinner at home, you may not have a choice. You could, of
course, decide not to eat, but that is another decision—i.e.,
not what to eat but whether or not to eat at all.

*A decision should not be confused with an outcome or
a result,* which is what occurs after you take action. A
decision is the act and an outcome is the result of that act.
The result might be expected or anticipated, but it might
also be something that you could not possibly predict. You
can control the way you make a decision but you cannot
control the results. Consequently, while a decision may
be well considered, it does not guarantee a good result.
You do not become clairvoyant when you become a skillful
decision-maker. What a good decision will do is give you

a better chance to get the result you want. So when you declare, "That was a great decision," you should be talking about how well you went about making the choice, rather than how the result appeared to you after the decision was made.

A decision also requires making some commitment of your resources—whether in terms of time, money, energy, or other things. If you're really interested in restructuring your life, you must give up some of your resources without a full guarantee that things will turn out the way you want them to.

Making a decision can be compared to painting a picture. The painter begins with an idea of what he hopes to create on the canvas. If he paints something he doesn't like, more is involved than simply starting over again. He has already committed his time, energies, paint, and canvas to the effort.

The painter, like people trying to create satisfying lives, has had to make a commitment of resources that he can never get back. As in life, he can choose to try again; he may alter the existing painting, making it more satisfactory; he may decide to live with what he has done; or he may even decide never to paint again. As in most decision situations, he has to determine what is most important to him before choosing what to do.

In the absence of guaranteed outcomes, many of us decide never to commit our resources. Consequently, our chances of painting satisfactory pictures of our lives are practically nil!

Little Decisions

What about those nagging little decisions that hang us up, in which the outcome hardly seems worth the time and energy spent deciding? Why do we have such a difficult, frustrating time with day-to-day choices: which suit to buy, whom to invite to the party, what to have for dinner, how to handle a phone request, where to spend the weekend?

While it might be argued that all of these choices could be very important under special conditions, normally they are not. And yet we agonize over them. These little decisions do have all the elements of a major decision, but they are different in one major respect: they are not critical enough to call for a long and involved decision-making process. In the absence of any process, however, these little decisions can become a hit-or-miss exercise, almost like flipping a coin, which doesn't convince the decider of the effectiveness of his choice. People in decision-making seminars sometimes declare that they prefer more difficult choices, because they can be more thorough and consequently more confident in the action they take.

But little decisions actually provide an excellent opportunity for you to learn about yourself and about what is involved in a choice. A nagging minor problem may be telling you something about what is important to you or may be related to a major issue in your life. The struggle over buying a suit may relate to anxiety about your appearance and what others think about it. Your debate over party invitations may show a concern about the quality of some friendships, or about your lack of self-confidence socially. So a good beginning point for dealing with the little decision is to try to identify the source of irritation. You might ask yourself why it is so difficult.

If you discover that the problem does have greater import for you than you first realized, you may want to spend more time on it. Once you've looked at the larger issues, reduce your decision to scale again. Now try to ascertain the *worst* thing that might happen if you make a certain choice. What would happen if you didn't invite one friend to your party and yet included others? Generally, you'll find that the worst thing that can happen isn't really so bad in the "little" decision situation. This should take some of the pressure off. What you are beginning to discover by looking at your choice in this way is that most decisions, even important ones, are not irreversible, and that you generally can manage the results of a little decision. You have also begun to deal with the crucial elements of all decisions—values, goals, alternatives, and outcomes.

Here are some other useful hints for handling little decisions:

1. *Be specific.* Try to develop a one-line statement about what you want the results of your decision to be. For example, "I want a suit I can wear with the accessories I already have."

2. *Set a time limit.* "If possible, I'm going to make a decision about my purchase within one hour."

3. *Know something about the possibilities before you begin looking.* "A blue suit will go with most of my shirts and ties."

4. *When you see something that will give you the results you want, stop looking.* "Somewhere there may be a better suit, but this is not a life-or-death matter. It is not worth trying to explore *all* of the possibilities."

5. *Make up your own mind; don't seek out excessive additional opinions.* The salesman may have good advice, but in the end you have to be comfortable with what you have chosen. You're buying the suit for yourself; nobody knows more about how you want to look and feel than you do.

6. *Note what you learned about yourself and about this decision.* The final results, good or bad, can contribute to the ability to make a better little decision next time.

You can learn what is involved in making a choice, you can define it, and you can think about it, but to make decisions effectively and coherently you will have to practice. To help you learn, I have provided exercises throughout the book, at each stage of the decision-making process. Becoming more conscious of how you go about making your everyday "little" decisions is itself a form of practice. Try the following questionnaire:

When you got up this morning to go about the day's tasks, what did you put on? Make a mental list (or write it down, if you prefer) of each item of clothing and each accessory.

Think about the *conscious* choices you made in dress as they apply to each of the following categories:

A. Weather.

B. How you felt this morning, both physically and mentally.

C. Things you had to do today.

D. People you expected to meet.

E. People you might run into.

Are you satisfied with your choices? Why or why not? Did you fail to dress adequately? Why? Were your decisions good or bad? Why?

What to wear may not be a critical decision every day. Can you think of any unusual situation when it might be a critical decision for you? What considerations tend to make the choice of apparel more important?

Did you learn anything about yourself in this exercise? Did you learn something about how you make decisions?

Some people steadfastly maintain that dressing isn't a decision-making process for them. But unless you have only one set of clothes available on a given morning, or you are compelled to wear a particular outfit (say, a uniform) for some reason, you do have to select. And if you think hard enough you'll find reasons for the selections you make. This exercise demonstrates the skills associated with everyday actions—determining what is important to you, what you want, how to act to get what you want, and what might happen if a certain course of action is selected.

The Critical Choice

If choosing what to wear is not an especially important or critical choice for you, can you recall a decision that was? It is important choices that cause most of us to feel the agony and anxiety that one of my mid-career clients described to me recently: "My problem in decision-making is anticipating and worrying about what can and will happen—I expend lots of energy in pre-worry."

Perhaps this is the way you feel when you face an important decision-making situation. Such a critical choice usually has the following four characteristics:

1. *It has some impact on your future.*
2. *It impacts on the lives of others.*
3. *It is important to you.*
4. *It requires time to reach.*

Think back over three critical decisions you've made in your life. Try to remember as fully as possible the circumstances, the pressures in your life at that time, what you were like as a person, how it felt to have this decision to make. Were you even aware that the decision *was* a critical one for you? Now write down each decision, and select from the list below the best description(s) of how you made it.

Decision #1 _____

_____

_____

Decision #2 _____

_____

_____

Decision #3 _____

_____

A. Took the safe way.
B. Let somebody else decide for me.
C. Used intuition; chose what I **felt** was right.
D. Consciously considered what was important, what I wanted, what the consequences might be.
E. Did what others expected.

_____ F. Took the first thing that came
_____   along.
G. Selected the most difficult
   because of the payoff.
H. Delayed deciding until something happened and other
   possibilities were gone.
I. Used some other approach
   (specify).

Are you satisfied with the outcomes of these decisions? Are you satisfied with how you went about making them? Perhaps your next critical decision, if made more carefully, can yield you more satisfaction on both counts.

Your Critical Decision

You may face a critical decision at this time that you could use this book to help you make. At the end of each chapter (and occasionally halfway through a particularly long chapter), I will give you an opportunity to examine this critical decision and to work through it as you learn and apply decision-making skills. Thus, as you read through the book, you will go through each phase of the decision-making process as it applies to a particular critical decision you need to make in your own personal life. Once you have selected the decision-making situation, try to answer the following preliminary questions:

1. What critical life choice are you facing now or do you expect to face in the near future?

2. Why is it critical?

3. What obstacles are in the way of your making this choice?

4. In what ways will the results of this choice (both positive and negative possibilities) affect your life?

5. In what ways will this choice get you closer to what you want in life?

6. *Why is what you want in this decision important to you?*

7. *At this point, what are some alternatives available to you?*

8. *When do you want to begin taking action?*

9. *How much risk, and what kind of risk, is involved?*

10. *Is the anticipated risk worth it? Why?*

3.
A Decision-Making Process That Works!

To be able to choose the line of greatest advantage instead of yielding in the path of least resistance . . . is the essence of freedom.
—George Bernard Shaw,
Man and Superman

Decisions that count in a positive way are those that bring about the most satisfying outcomes possible in your life. While there are many ways to go about making choices, the process outlined in this book is designed to take into consideration and preserve your uniqueness, so that your decisions will reflect what you want the form of your life to be. This process applies equally to decisions relating to personal, educational, or career situations.

A model for critical decision-making appears on pages 23–25. Before examining it, though, you need to be aware of some of the general assumptions associated with this model:

1. Most people do have an opportunity to make choices and take action within their present setting.

2. Decision-making is a process involving skills that can be learned for use in real-life situations.

3. These skills can be refined as you practice them in simulated and actual decision situations.

4. Unlike decisions made in a laboratory setting, each decision you make is unique in a number of ways. This is due primarily to changes and uncertainties that relate to you, to the people around you, and to the setting in which you make each choice.

5. Most good things in life happen because we have a hand in making them happen. Usually the best chance you'll ever have of getting what you want is by going after it.

6. You probably have more going for you in terms of personal assets, talent, resources, and experience than you know right now.

7. You'll probably never know all of the possibilities that exist in a given situation, and most likely you'll never be able to get complete information about any single possibility.

8. Most people do not know what values are really important to them.

9. Personal values are learned. They may change and be reordered in terms of priority throughout your life.

10. You have to learn what you want in life before you can make well-considered, well-informed choices.

11. Decision-making is an ongoing process. Once you make a decision, you are not done with it. You become responsible not only for the results but also for dealing with the impact it might have on other choices.

Underlying the success of the decision-making model is the assumption that you care enough about your life to do something about it. Learning and applying a decision-making process is hard work. There is no simple formula, and there are no guarantees. But properly executed decision-making gives you direction and a much better chance to get the best of what there is for you.

Chuck is an example of a person who cared enough about his life to apply the decision-making model. As a rising executive in a large accounting firm, Chuck faced a difficult choice for himself and his family: whether or not to take a year off and travel, using their existing savings. Chuck's two children, who did average to above-average work in school, would be entering the eighth and tenth grades the following year. Chuck and his wife attached a high value to travel, and they thought there might not be a more opportune time for such a trip, since the children were just beginning to be involved in the social scene at school and the older one was getting close to college preparation time. As Chuck worked through the decision-making model, these were some of the entries he made:

Decision setting: It is more common for a person to take off now, but I'm uncertain as to how the company would react. I have bounced the idea off a few friends, but they think going for a whole year is a bit too much. If we're going to be able to do it for a year, this is the best time, what with the kids getting more involved with social events and sports teams, and with Jim moving closer to college.

Goals: My family wants to go, and one of our highest values is associated with doing and learning together. I think travel is the best way to achieve this. I have ample savings for the trip, but it will take away from what I have put aside to date for my children's education. Even so, this contributes to the goal of promoting growth for all of us. On the other hand, it may well prove to be an obstacle in moving along the promotion line in my firm. I do have skills that are in demand—accounting—so I could get another job and probably a good one if I had to. Over-riding the situation is the feeling I have that if we don't do this now, we'll probably not get a chance to do it as a family in the future.

Working goal statement: I want to provide myself and

my family with a learning and growth experience that we can share at a significant point in our lives.

Most important information considerations: My whole family wants this; it may be a unique opportunity in terms of all of our lives. The time seems right. I might jeopardize my career. I have ample savings to do this.

Alternatives at this time: Take a year off. Do this some other time. Travel as a family for two months in the summer, using my vacation time. Take a short leave for two months. Forget the whole notion.

What additional information do I need? Check with my boss to ascertain his attitude and get a better sense of my future when I return. Find out how this would affect the kids in terms of schooling. Test the job market in case I need to look before we leave in order to have something in place when I get back.

Thus Chuck was on his way to making a well-considered, well-informed choice. As it turned out, he was not encouraged to take the year off by his company, and this turned out to be the highest area of risk that he had to deal with. For the rest of his family, the problems were minimal—in fact, the school authorities suggested that this would be a great educational experience for the children and it was probably the best time to do it.

As Chuck reassessed his values, he felt that the trip would be worth the risk involved in perhaps losing his job or being slowed down in terms of future promotions. He felt that the worst thing that could happen would be to lose his job, and he assessed the probability of this as unlikely after talking with his boss. He also felt that the cost of the trip would have the highest payoff for everybody if it involved a whole year instead of several months. To protect himself regarding a possible loss of job, Chuck decided to look at some other job opportunities that he might be able to pick up upon his return. As an experienced and successful accountant, he found that the probability of landing a new position was good. Consequently, Chuck decided to take the year off and travel with his family.

Now look at the model for critical decision-making carefully and try to follow Chuck's decision process as you examine it.

A MODEL FOR CRITICAL DECISION-MAKING

Phase I
Becoming Aware of Your Choices

The Decision Situation

What decision do I face?

Am I aware that I have a choice?

Phase II
Discovering the Uniqueness of Your Situation

A. The Decision Setting

What conditions seem to be imposed on my decision by:

1. Changing circumstances and attitudes of society?
2. Uncertainty?
3. Limitations in myself and imposed by my environment?
4. "Luck"?
5. Social and personal pressures?
6. Time pressures?

B. You and Your Goals

> What personal characteristics and abilities make me unique?
>
> What assets and/or liabilities do I bring to the situation?
>
> What experiences, attitudes, interests, or beliefs do I bring to my decision?
>
> What are my personal values? What is most important to me, and how willing am I to commit myself to it?
>
> What are my goals in life? Short-term? Long-term? How does this decision relate to my goals?
>
> What obstacles might keep me from reaching my goals?

C. Working Goal Statement for This Decision

> What do I want? (A brief statement reflecting the most important information about me and my decision setting that will answer the question What do I want?)
>
> Then move on to alternative development.

Phase III

Finding the Best Alternative for You

> Most important information considerations thus far in this decision based on the setting, myself, my goals, and my statement of what I want.

> What is the most complete list of alternatives I can develop at this time?

> What additional information do I need to check on these alternatives and develop others?

What do I need to get this information?

1. People to see and talk to.
2. Things to read and research.
3. Experiences needed.
4. Self-knowledge required.

Selective list of my most promising alternatives, based on more complete information.

Phase IV
Predicting
and Weighing
the Risks

What do I know about the outcomes of my possible alternatives?
Alternatives
  Possible results of choosing this alternative
  Probability of these results
  Desirability of these results

What is the balance of probability and desirability in my final decision formula?

Is the risk worth taking? Why?

Phase V
Taking Action

What is the one best alternative for me?

What is keeping me from acting on it **NOW**?

Phase VI
Being
Responsive
to Your
Choice

Responsibilities resulting from my action.

Did I make any mistakes in this decision that I would like to correct in the future:
  In terms of the decision process?
  In terms of unexpected negative outcomes?

What New Decisions Am I Now in a Position to Make?

Don't be put off by the detail in the chart. This model assumes that you are starting from point zero and it takes you through a total process that optimizes your choices of getting what you want. As you begin to apply parts of the process and as your skills improve, you will find that there are a lot of valid shortcuts. You may already be well through Phases I and II for some decisions, while for others you may need to go through the entire process quite carefully. Moreover, there will be some decision situations where you will not have the time, the need, or the inclination to apply the entire process. But if you do skip part of the process, be sure you know how you went about making your choice so that you can profit from an evaluation of the experience.

This model is set up so that you can go back and revise various parts of your information as you move toward a decision to act on. In fact, a review of the elements is valuable in double-checking each stage of the process.

The chapters that follow will take up each phase of the decision-making process in sequence. At the end of each chapter, you will return to your own critical decision, exploring it step by step to the final action you decide to take. Along the way, you will be developing a number of decision-making skills that can be applied to any important decision you may make later on. You will learn to:

1. Become aware of when you have a choice and when those choices are in danger of being forfeited.

2. Become aware of the forces and pressures relating to yourself, others, and your environment that may affect your decision.

3. Measure your assets and liabilities accurately.

4. Clarify what you want.

5. Assess your alternatives.

6. Relate what is important for you to the available possibilities.

7. Exercise your rights as a decider (listed on p. 150).

8. Assume the responsibility for your actions and for dealing effectively with their results.

In sum, the process begins with caring and the awareness that your life may be better if you do something about it. The starting point is *you*, your feelings, your values, your experiences, your attitudes. You will discover many things about yourself and the world about you. You will find that your preferences are being painted into the picture of your life—and that more and more you will want the responsibility for determining what the final portrait will be.

Your Critical Decision

Take a moment to go back to the critical decision that you would like this book to help you with. Read over the decision-making model and identify those areas that you think will have to be clarified, developed, or studied further before you can make this decision yield the results you want.

As an additional exercise, consider a recent or past decision that you have made. With this decision in mind, review the phases of the model and try to determine how close the process you used in an important decision was to what is outlined in the model.

4.

Becoming Aware of
Your Choices

Many men go fishing all of their lives without knowing it is not the fish they are after.
—Henry David Thoreau

Many opportunities to make decisions present themselves
to us throughout a lifetime. Some people avail themselves
of these opportunities. Others do not. Those who fail to
make choices when they have the opportunity are not
necessarily backing away from the choices. *They may
simply not recognize that a choice does exist.* In fact, in an
increasingly complex society the number of people who
are aware of the choices available to them continues to
diminish.

This all too common state of unawareness has a number
of important implications. In the first place, it means that
you may not be taking action when it is possible; therefore your chances for moving in the direction you desire
are diminished. Second, by not taking action you are
giving up some of the precious control you have over
your life. Third, by reducing the number of times you
make choices you are likely to forfeit the chances to
increase your decision-making ability and skills. Finally,
with diminishing awareness of the possible decisions, you
will tend to let others decide when you have a choice.
This is tantamount to letting others run your life.

It is easy to understand why people are willing to forfeit their freedom in what they may perceive as an unmanageable world. You yourself can sense this helplessness when you appear to be pushed into a course of action without really making a decision. A job offer may carry with it a sizable salary increase over your current salary, yet the job isn't as exciting or challenging as your current job. In the end you go with the higher salary. Are you really making a decision in this case, or are you bending to the pressures and value systems of our society, which tells us that money is more important than job satisfaction?

This kind of pressure can lead to a point where you will no longer even try to make decisions. Alvin Toffler comments, in his perceptive account of the changes wrought in our lives by technology, *Future Shock*: "The society of the future will consist of adults who opt out of choice . . . who let others make decisions for them." The tragedy here is that no matter who makes the decision, you have to live with that choice. Whether we admit it or not, many of us are living this way right now. Examples of this type of behavior are legion, including individuals of all ages and levels of education and affluence.

How many times have we heard ourselves or others say: "Why am I going to college?" "I hate my job, but what can I do?" "I know it's a bad relationship, but I'm afraid to do anything about it." These statements speak to the fears and problems many of us have in making up our minds. They reflect an unwillingness to take control of our lives. The battle for control begins with a struggle between you and *everything* around you. It's a struggle for what your life will become. To find out now where you stand in this battle, study the statements below and circle the one in each pair that represents what you believe to be true.

1. a. Most of the good things in life are the result of luck.
   b. Good things most always result from some action you take.
2. a. What is going to happen will happen.
   b. You can have a definite impact on most things that happen in your life.
3. a. Success results from being in the right place at the right time.
   b. Success results from hard work.
4. a. There is little the individual can do about what is happening in the world around him.
   b. The little guy *can* fight City Hall effectively.
5. a. It is not a good idea to plan too far ahead.
   b. You may not be able to see the future, but you can have something to do with what it can be.
6. a. What happens to me is really up to a larger social order.
   b. What happens to me is mostly my own doing.

If most of your answers were in the "a" category, you tend to feel that your life is controlled by external forces. You may, then, want to think about what it takes to bring more internal control to your decisions and to your life.

When I talk about gaining control in your life, I'm not talking about controlling the outcomes of your decisions. Outcomes are always subject to uncertainties and changes that cannot be predicted in advance with absolute surety. What I do mean is getting a clearer idea of what you want in life and moving toward it by developing viable alternatives.

You have probably heard people exclaim that they have little or no choice in life. Perhaps you have thought this true of yourself. This sense of powerlessness oftens stems from the complexities of our age that make the world and life itself appear more and more unmanageable. True, there may appear to be some movement, the semblance of action being taken, in the life of an unaware individual, but it is probably along prescribed paths. The most frightening aspect of this kind of behavior is that the more common it gets, the more difficult it becomes to recognize our real opportunities for taking action. People will tend to do less reaching for what they want, thus severely reducing any chance of attaining their real potential. The chance to practice and develop decision-making skills is reduced dramatically until the whole process runs full cycle—less skillful decision-makers become more and more apprehensive about taking action even when it is recognized as a possibility. We need little imagination to predict the devastating outcomes of decisionless lives.

Awareness of choice begins with an awareness of self and of what you want in life. First you need to become sensitive to the fact that something is interfering with your attempt to get what you want. When you feel or observe this point of interference, you can take action to deal with it—or you can let it frustrate your attempt to define yourself and to attain what you want.

It is very unusual to be able to say with accuracy, "There is no choice in this situation." Choice practically always exists. All that is required is another course of action. You may not like that action, but it *is* an alternative and should be recognized as such. A person falsely accused of a crime may plead guilty to a lesser charge because he doesn't want to face the possibility of being found guilty if his case goes to trial. In this instance the potentially negative consequences appear so overwhelming that there seems to be no choice. Yet in this example, as in many other critical decisions, there *is* a choice and, more than likely, there are other options that go unexplored because the decider is not aware a choice is possible.

One way to increase your awareness of choice is to try

to think of all the things you might do in any situation that seems to be interfering with your getting what you want. Begin by building as many possible actions as you can without evaluating them in any way. At first you may be inclined to reject something right away as being unacceptable or impossible. Resist this impulse. Don't set anything aside without a second—or third—look. All too frequently we anticipate negative consequences of new or different actions without taking the time to look for the positives. The falsely accused person opting for a trial may go to jail, but he may also go free.

Even before you start thinking about possible consequences, develop a sense of the range of actions available to you. By doing this, you become aware that there *are* choices—probably many of them. Even more important, you are building a storehouse of alternatives that may serve you well in the future. Finally, by rejecting the "no choice" attitude you can begin to apply and refine your decision-making skills.

What are some specific things you can do to increase your awareness of choice? First, open your mind. Begin thinking for yourself. Ask yourself, "What can I do if I don't have to think about any consequences at all?" Fantasize a little. Write down the things you think are possible and even impossible to do in the given decision situation.

Suppose your relationship with your spouse is the problem. There are a number of actions you could take that might seem possible or impossible for you, as follows:

Appear Possible	Appear Impossible
Talk it out	Leave home
Therapy (family, couple, or individual)	Have an affair
Divorce and marry again	Ignore spouse
Separation	Physical fight

Others: Others:

_____   _____
_____   _____
_____   _____

Add more actions to each list or change the entries around in each column to suit you. You'll begin to realize that there are many actions available, and you could choose practically any of them if you did not have to worry about the consequences. Of course, somewhere along the line you *will* worry about the consequences, but that should be done after you've recognized that you do have a choice. *There is more than one course of action available to you.*

Apply this procedure to a situation you are facing or have faced recently where you thought you had no choice. If you have trouble coming up with possible actions, ask a friend for suggestions. Chances are that input from another person will serve as a stimulus and help you to think of other actions on your own.

A No-Choice Situation _____
_____
_____

Why You Thought There Were No Choices Available _____
_____
_____

Possibilities That You Can Now Identify as Alternative Choices
_____
_____

The Path of Least Resistance

As millions of us have done in the past, you probably moved on to either college or a job after high school without ever really considering any other course of action. Who made the decision? Did you, or did your parents? Was it a decision, or was it the tremendous pressure that seemed to move you without your having actually considered the available options? There are so many forces pushing people in certain well-defined directions that you may think you *decided* to go in that direction when in reality you did not.

The whole process is analogous to falling into a river where the current is moving swiftly. It's so easy just to let it push you along. But as you move, the current gets stronger. The effort to take a few strokes toward shore produces very little progress and proves tiring, so you decide to let the stream take you along for a bit more just to see what is around the bend. When you round the bend, the current is even stronger and you see that you're heading for a waterfall. Now it's too late to escape the waterfall and a tragic crash to the rocks below.

Taking the path of least resistance in life can also lead to a point where it is unlikely that you can change direction and avoid the falls. Today, more than ever, it is vital to exercise your freedom. You can always choose the mainstream. But the person who fights the current and gets closer to where he wants to be is the one who is apt to come up with the superior result—even though it will take a little more work initially. The reluctance to make this initial effort is what tends to cut down your awareness of available, and sometimes advantageous, alternatives in a difficult decision situation.

In my seminars, I work with many bright, affluent high-school juniors and seniors. One of the decision-making exercises I run them through goes as follows. First I ask them what they plan to do after high school. Virtually all of them say they are going on to college. Then I ask them what other alternatives they have considered. In group after group, many of these talented youngsters have not considered any other alternative. They have moved toward college without really making a decision. Recall our definition of a decision: choosing between two or more courses of action. These students have not considered other alternatives, and consequently they have not made a choice. They really don't know if college is the best option among several available to them.

Next I ask the students to develop options other than college. After the initial paralysis wears off, they come up with literally dozens of possibilities. Recently, I wrote all of the options a group developed on the chalk board. Then I asked for comments. One young woman said, "These possibilities look like a lot of fun." Another student added, "And most of them are very respectable." Another noted that even without college you could become a highly educated person. Now, I'm not saying that college would not be the best choice for most of these students. But I am saying that other options would be more appropriate for some of them. And for all of the students a well-considered choice requires a careful look at the alternatives. When you weigh alternatives against each other, you gain a better sense of what the results might be for a variety of available courses of action. You then have a far better chance of being satisfied with your choice. Even if you go with the mainstream, you will feel different knowing you have actively chosen it, rather than simply being swept along.

From now on when you hear someone say, "I didn't have any other choice," or "There was no choice in the matter," become especially alert and even suspicious. When anyone—a parent, your boss, your child, your spouse, your own inner voice—tries to tell you that there is but one course of action available to you, contest the statement. Remember that you're the one who has to live with the consequences. It is *your* commitment in time, energy, and resources. It is *your* life!

The "Have To" Dilemma

All through your life you have been making choices. Some, perhaps very important to you at one time, may now have become routine, even automatic, not requiring much thought. Others you are more aware of as choices, those which could be easily reversed or made over again with little cost to you. Still others involve significant consequences for you, your future, and other people. These are your critical choices.

All these decisions, whether routine or critical, have one thing in common. They must offer you a choice between two or more alternative actions. It is easy to lose sight of these alternatives by assuming a "have to" situation.

Some people claim they "have to" get up in the morning and go to work in order to support themselves or their families. But they do have a choice. They can choose to stay in bed and not go to work. For most of us, going to work is an automatic decision, one we resolved a long time ago and to which we can now respond without consciously making a choice. You may even have thought about the results of not going to work, and the prospects— not being able to support your family, losing your job security, or giving up an activity you enjoy—are simply too unappealing when weighed against going to work. But, however unappealing, the options are there. Although it is rarely admitted, attendance records in all areas of work tend to show the highest absenteeism on Fridays and Mondays. So it would appear that at least some people are making the other choice.

There are other situations that people do not think involve choices that can forever prevent them from closing the gap between what they have and what they want in life. Many married women have told me that whether or not to go back to college was not a choice for them because they "had to" raise their children first. An older man confided that he could not pursue what he really wanted because he was too close to retirement and he "had to" keep at what he was doing to get all of his benefits. One woman told me that she could not pursue a career because her husband was about to be transferred; she thought she had no choice because she "had to" consider her husband's career first.

Without being aware of it, each of these people felt what every decision-maker experiences in a critical situation: conflict. A critical decision typically involves conflict, which requires some resolution of what is important to you, what you want, and how much you are willing to risk to get it. In the examples above, the expectations of society or of relatives or close associates of the people involved were overpowering enough to limit the exploration of the available options.

As you become a more skillful decision-maker, you will learn to deal with this conflict so that the best possible outcome accrues to you. You will learn to consider the other options and the possible results of those options before you say you "have to" stay home to raise the children, reject the possibility of a new career after age fifty-five, or give up your career because of your mate's.

Alice Henderson, the woman who had a career conflict with her husband, David, finally did explore the possibilities. Her first step was to discuss her problem with David—which she had never done! The two of them went over the situation for many hours and came up with an alternative satisfactory to both. David was surprised that his wife felt so strongly about pursuing her interests. It was his knowledge of alternatives in the business world that helped Alice find a viable option that reduced the conflict for both of them. The field that interested her, career counseling in an educational setting, tended to require full-time work, and opportunities were very limited. When her husband suggested that there was a need for her kind of skills in business settings, she decided to focus on that area and to get additional training in organizational development. This, coupled with her counseling skills, equipped her for a career with both full- and part-time job opportunities and in a field where she could take advantage of her husband's business contacts. But many people, unaware that a choice exists, never begin to discuss the problem or how they feel about it. Others—and their numbers are vast—do not express their feelings and opinions even when they know a decision is very important to them.

Take a moment to think about your own life. What are some of the things you'd like to do that you think you can't do because you simply "have to" do something else. List some of those "have to" situations below. For instance, "I want to write a novel but I have to support my family."

"Have To" Situations

_____

_____

_____

_____

When you have completed this exercise, you have begun to establish specific things that are important to you in your life today. In addition, you can begin to sense the conflicts that will need to be resolved if you are to move toward what you want. And you have also begun to become aware of the fact that you do have a choice.

Who or What Controls Your Life

Many people yield control of their lives to others. They let the expectations or needs or demands of others dictate and limit the actions they themselves might have been able to take. Sometimes they never even realize that this is going on; other times they accept it as the norm.

A woman in one of my decision-making classes told me that in twenty-five years of marriage she never controlled the time she went to bed. She said that after dinner she and her husband would usually read or watch television. When her husband decided to put down his newspaper or book, or stop watching television, he would simply announce, "Well, I guess it's time to go to bed." The woman became increasingly annoyed at this and finally decided to discuss her annoyance with her husband. She told him that she was not always ready for bed when he was, that occasionally she preferred to continue her reading or viewing. She suggested that she could decide for herself when she wanted to go to bed, even if it meant that they might sometimes have different bedtimes.

In a very modest way, this woman was trying to gain some control over her life, attempting to move toward what *she* wanted. As it happened, the particular problem was symptomatic of other, more basic conflicts in their marriage, and they subsequently decided on a divorce. The important point to remember here is that when you decide to take control of your life there will be some cost involved, both in terms of making the effort to take control and in what might result from that effort. In this case, one of the results of the effort was the severing of a relationship—which may or may not have been expected when this woman took the initial step toward gaining some control.

Taking control is even more difficult in situations where we can't clearly identify who—or what—is doing the controlling. It can sometimes seem as futile as "fighting City Hall." Too often people assume that some omnipresent, all-powerful "they" is in control. It's "they" who cause traffic jams, overtax us, don't pick up the garbage, never come on time to repair the refrigerator, overbook hotels so we don't have a room even though we made a reservation.

Suppose you're in the airport waiting to board a flight when "they" announce a "short" delay. Hours later, grumbling and wondering when you'll be on your way, you hear the announcement again. While this situation may seem to lack any control possibilities, there are actions that can be taken. For one thing, you can address very specific questions to the airline personnel. For example: Tell me all you definitely know about this flight and its expected departure. Is the aircraft scheduled to make the flight physically here? If not, where is the replacement aircraft coming from?

Depending on the responses you get, you can begin to formulate alternative plans of action. If you find the airline agent doesn't know anything for sure or that the aircraft has not yet arrived, it's probably a good idea to look for another flight, because the delay is apt to be long. By getting this information early, you can line up a number of other possibilities. But if you let too much time go by, those alternatives start to disappear. Another flight on a different airline may become filled to capacity because some of the other people waiting from your flight have already switched. If there is no other flight, that still does not mean you have lost total control of the situation. You might decide to have a leisurely meal, read a book in the comfort of the cocktail lounge, or even revise your flight plans so you can spend a pleasant evening in the city and depart the next morning.

The sad truth of the matter is that most people do assume they have no control in such a situation and simply wait it out, frustrated by the lack of information and physically uncomfortable sitting around the waiting lounge.

As you begin to gain control over your life, you will reduce your use of the word "they," because you will begin to find out where to go to get action or satisfaction. "They" will become people or situations you can identify with some specificity.

Taking control, I repeat, does involve some risks. You have no guarantee of getting what you want. For example, if you switch flights, the next flight may also be delayed. Or your original flight may be ready for boarding moments after you switch to one that will not depart for two hours. So while you cannot *guarantee* the best outcome for yourself by taking control—there are seldom any guarantees—you do begin to get a hold on the situation on your own terms. *Your* time and resources are being spent under the conditions *you* prescribe. You have begun to make things happen, and regardless of outcome, you have removed much of the discomfort of operating under the cloud of total uncertainty that exists when one simply waits for things to happen. The tactics will prove useful in future situations.

Taking control also means committing your resources to a course of action. If you make a reservation on a second flight, your reservation on the first will be canceled, making that alternative no longer available to you.

You may also get results that you don't expect. One man who travels extensively on business has waged an aggressive war to gain control over what might appear to be noncontrollable situations. When he reaches the hotel registration desk and is told that no rooms are available—even though he has a reservation—his response is simply to ask the clerk to point him to the lobby. He explains that is where he is going to unpack his bags, put on his pajamas, and retire for the night on one of the couches—until he gets the room he reserved. So far, this courageous soul has been a hundred percent successful in getting a room. Of course, in another set of circumstances other outcomes could occur as well, including being trotted off to a room in the local jail. The occasional negative result, however, usually appears small in light of the success this person has achieved in taking control of a disagreeable situation.

I was caught recently in a similar situation. Returning from Puerto Rico with my family after a very enjoyable holiday, I arrived at the airport two hours before flight time with tickets in hand. The lines were long. Over an hour later, when I was able to check in at the counter for our seating assignments, I was told that the flight had no space and we would have to wait for the next flight, due to depart several hours later.

Although I had no knowledge of what the law might be in this situation, I did feel that I had been mistreated and I was determined to do something about it. I asked for the man in charge. When I was ushered into his office, I asked him two questions: "Do you think this is a good practice for an airline?" and "Is it legal?" After a bit of verbal fencing, he presented me with a check representing a full refund for myself and the five other members of my family, and we were booked without charge on the very next flight. Subsequently, I found out that while airlines can overbook, by law they do have to get you on a flight within a prescribed period of time or else you are entitled to ride free. By making the effort to control an apparently uncontrollable situation, I found out information that will be very valuable in the future, and the unexpected free flight put a fitting cap on our holiday.

In the space below, try to recall problem situations in which you thought you had no control and consequently did nothing about them. Then try to think of any kind of action you might have taken—regardless of the effort involved or the possible risk you might have incurred.

**Situations in Which You
Thought You Had No Control**   **Things You Could Have Done**

_____	_____
_____	_____
_____	_____
_____	_____

What did you learn? For many of us, simply thinking about such situations leads us to realization of at least one thing we might do to gain more control.

As you review your answers above, consider the broader question, "Who or what tends to control my life?" Respond to this question generally and then more specifically, relating it to the major decision areas of your life: work, education, leisure, personal relationships, and self-satisfaction. Write down your responses.

Who or what tends to control your life? _____

_____

_____

For each of the major areas of your life (work, education, leisure, etc.) in whom or what is the main locus of control? _____

_____

_____

Your Critical Decision

How did you become aware that you had a choice?

What is the choice?

Are you assuming that you "have to" decide a certain way?

What do others want you to do?

How does what you have learned in the past tend to dictate your choice?

What current social trends are influencing your thinking?

What "controllers" might you have to deal with in this critical decision?

5.

The Decision Setting

All decisions boil down to a choice among
alternatives of what is most valued for whatever reasons and are determined by the
particular value system that prevails.
—R. W. Sperry, *American Psychologist*,
April 1977

One of the many aspects of life that you must contend
with is that things are going to change in various ways
from year to year, from month to month, and even from
day to day. This is true especially when you examine the
setting in which you make decisions. Regardless of what
kind of decision you face, you will always be dealing with
a dynamic and somewhat unpredictable situation. Personal
and social change, uncertainty, limitations and pressure, as
well as luck and time limits, all play a part. Recognizing
and understanding these elements in each situation is
essential to sound decision-making.

Change

The most fundamental element in the dynamic environment of choice is change. Your own changes, as well as
those occurring around you, have impact on you as the
individual making the decision. Not too long ago, for
example, divorce was still frowned upon as an alternative
to an unsatisfactory marriage. Divorced people were not
readily "accepted" by society, and divorced men and

women found their social lives appreciably affected. Divorced women experienced special difficulties; for instance, they could not get credit or even maintain their charge cards in their own names. While some of these problems still exist, general attitudes have now changed and laws have been instituted to protect the rights of divorcees. Divorce is probably now more palatable as an alternative to a poor relationship.

An infinite number of such changes are taking place in the world today. Some of the most publicized concern attitudes toward abortion, single parenting, the value of a college education, equality of opportunity, and environmental protection. These shifting attitudes provide you with options that never before existed.

Consider the person deciding on the purchase of a car— a decision that from a financial standpoint often ranks second only to buying a home. The factors affecting that decision today are different from those of even five years ago. Gasoline is more expensive. Automobiles are more expensive. It doesn't seem as necessary or even appropriate to have a luxury automobile that consumes large amounts of gasoline. There is less social pressure to buy a new car every two or three years, or to have several cars in one's driveway. And in the eyes of some, it is almost unpatriotic to drive an uneconomical vehicle.

Suppose your own priorities for an automobile have not changed. You are still looking for comfort and safety when you drive—and you want a large American car. In this case, the changes you observe around you may affect your choice. Will there be sufficient gas available to run this car? Will the new attitudes bring about changes in the laws so that your new car will be taxed as a "gas guzzler"? Are you willing to pay increased costs to get what you want?

Each decision, then, must be examined in light of your own needs, as well as the social and physical environment in which you live. To get a better grasp on the changes in the world around you, complete the following exercise. Look at some of the major social concerns reflected on the front page of your city newspaper. How do they differ from the concerns of five years ago? How do they relate to your own life and the important decisions you currently face?

Major Social Issues Today (Rank from 1 to 5 in order of importance for you now)	**How You Would Have Ranked Them Five Years Ago**
Crime	_____
Abortion	_____
Honesty in government	_____
Tax inequalities	_____
Busing	_____
Women's liberation	_____
Energy conservation	_____
Unemployment	_____

You may find that some of today's issues did not exist five years ago. If that is so, simply indicate that it is a new concern related to your decision-making environment. Go one step further and consider how these new issues affect your important choices.

Issue	**Effect on Your Choices**
For example: Unemployment	Reluctance to change jobs or search for better alternative.
_____	_____
_____	_____
_____	_____
_____	_____

You can see how important the changes around you are. Equally important, however, are the changes within yourself. You may have recently acquired new skills or interests, or perhaps developments in your life make it important to consider taking new action. Even if you're content with your current course, you may feel it's time to pursue it more intensely. Examine your life and the changes in it. This is vital if you want to progress to a desirable goal.

Discovering how you have changed is no easy task. Some things are fairly obvious and you can spot them. Occasionally, other people will mention differences they've noticed in you. To complete the picture, you can begin by taking a hard and honest look at your life as it was several years ago—and as it is now. Try to recall the things you preferred to do five or more years ago and then think of the things you prefer to do now. In the self-inventory below, write down some of your preferences, including work, leisure activities, hobbies, and volunteer efforts.

Things You Preferred to Do Five Years Ago

Things You Prefer to Do Now

_____   _____
_____   _____
_____   _____
_____   _____
_____   _____

What changes do you observe? Why have these changes occurred? Have you developed new skills, interests, or concerns? Are there different people you have to consider? How has the changing world around you affected your preferences? Write down some changes in your life that account for these differences.

_____
_____
_____

When you have had time to digest this, take it one step further and rank your preferences. Put a "1" next to your first preference five years ago and rank the remaining items in descending order. Do the same for the present preferences. What do you observe? Most people see some change in order of preference even if the same activities occur on each list.

This analysis of the influence of change in your life should make it clear that you cannot make a well-considered choice in a vacuum. As *you* change, so do the considerations you have to take into account before you make a choice. The factor of change also makes it important for you to frequently reevaluate decisions you have already made, because each ensuing decision should be considered in an accurate perspective.

Uncertainty

Another factor to be considered in the dynamic world of choice is that of uncertainty. It is rare—in fact, it is virtually impossible—for you to be able to predict with absolute certainty the results of any critical choice. "Anything can happen," the expression goes, and indeed it can! The most highly qualified people may not be admitted to the colleges of their choice, receive the promotions they have their hearts set on, or get the jobs they apply for. Or they may in fact attain what they desire, and then find themselves faced with totally un-expected results. In other words, a good decision does not guarantee a good result.

Here is a case in point. Roger and Ann wanted to buy a house. They were very clear on the kind of community in which they wanted to live and they spent several years searching for the community and house that would satisfy their desires. They finally made a well-informed, well-considered decision. Then, less than a year after they moved in, their new community's zoning laws were changed to allow commercial enterprises to operate within the confines of the town. This change deeply affected the couple's environment and happiness. Thus an unknown factor had adversely affected the results of their carefully thought out decision.

Who can predict what the economy will be like in five years, whether one of your loved ones might contract a terminal illness, or how technological advances may affect a relatively secure job picture? But as an individual making decisions, what you can and must do is make every attempt to *reduce* the degree of uncertainty involved in your course of action. This does not mean that you must always choose the more certain course of action. Rather, it means locating the uncertainty involved and taking it into consideration before you decide. Later I'll discuss some ways to deal with and reduce uncertainty. But, even at best, you will normally have to choose a course of action whose results are not entirely sure. This is one of the major obstacles that prevent people from making decisions.

It may help to remember that uncertainty affects not just new decisions but the course of action you're currently pursuing as well—one that may seem comfortably familiar and secure. Suppose, for example, you receive a very tempting job offer. It pays more than your present position and will give you an opportunity to pursue your career goals. However, you like your current job and especially your boss, who has supported your efforts and has promoted you at a rapid rate. While the new offer is attractive, you're not sure you'll like your work with a new firm. You're even less certain about the prospects of working for a new boss. Taking all these factors into account, you elect to stay in your present position. Less than a month after you have made your decision, your boss takes another job and you don't like his replacement at all.

One of the best ways to gain a sense of the uncertainty involved in your alternatives is to try some practice decision situations. *Fantasize* with me for a moment. You have just returned home to find an official-looking letter. It informs you that you can no longer follow whatever your principal occupation is at the time—be it business-man, housewife, professional, or student. Given this situation, what would you do?

After recovering from the shock, think of all the things you *could* do to earn a living. Remember, that's *could* do. They don't have to be things that you would like to do, or that you might have to do forever, or even that you're currently qualified to do. They are simply things you *could* pursue, given the fact that you can no longer do what you've been doing. Write down all the possibilities.

_____	_____
_____	_____
_____	_____
_____	_____

Make your list specific. Each thing you write down should be an occupation that has the potential of provid-ing you with a living and/or other important satisfactions.

After you have done this, assess each in terms of the uncertainty involved. Start by saying, "If I did this, what might result? How sure am I that it would result?"

As you tried to complete the list, what did you think about? Was it easy to make the list? If it was difficult, what made it so? Some people have trouble responding to this situation because they can't think of other things they might be able to do. Others find it difficult because family responsibilities make certain occupations impossible. Still

Things I Could Do	What Might Result	What Uncertainties Are Involved
Example: Convert a hobby into a business.	More satisfaction with what I'm doing.	Will somebody buy my product?
	Much less income to start.	What future events might lead to failure?
		What chance is there for success in the next five years?
_____	_____	_____
_____	_____	_____
_____	_____	_____

others put down only those things they are *certain* they could do; as a result, many possibilities go unlisted. Some feel they're simply not qualified to do anything except what they are doing now. This in itself is anxiety-producing. But one of the key "limiters" of all attempts to compile a list is the uncertainty we read into each entry. What uncertainties have you associated with the items on your list? Why do some seem more uncertain than others? How sure are you that this perceived uncertainty is real?

Now let's go a few steps further. From your list try to determine the three occupations you'd be most likely to pursue. Circle them. Why did you choose them? What might happen if you pursued these options? Do they all have the same general degree and kind of uncertainty?

This is a useful exercise that you can apply to many situations: planning a trip, applying for a variety of jobs, considering retirement plans, or even organizing a party. Obviously, it is a great help to be able to decrease the uncertainty—or at least to be sure of the degree of uncertainty involved. This requires mastering additional skills so that you can: know what is important to you, find appropriate information, and be aware of risks you might be willing to take. We'll get to these skills in the following chapters.

The goal here is to learn how to avoid decision paralysis when you are faced with some degree of uncertainty. Many people I work with, especially adolescents, see such a confusing, uncertain future ahead that they ask, "What's the use of making plans or of taking action based on all the uncertainty out there?" Obviously, we cannot control the future. But we *can* take action now to try to achieve results closer to what we want them to be. If we don't try at all, one thing *is* certain: We'll have *no* say in our future.

Limitations

A third major factor in all decision situations is limitation —personal and social. Not that limitations will keep you from attaining your goals. Quite the contrary! Once you recognize them clearly, you have taken the first crucial step toward overcoming or avoiding them. By defining your limitations, you will also be able to see your assets more clearly—all the things you have going for you.

Personal limitations include all those qualities, characteristics, skills, abilities, achievements, attitudes, feelings, and personal resources that you lack—or that you may simply *think* you lack! Other limitations are imposed on you by the society in which you live. These might include growing up in a family that cannot afford to send you to college, being a woman in a primarily male occupation such as banking, or being of a certain racial or ethnic origin. The number of these limitations is infinite and constantly changing. All of us have some limitations, which we must recognize and deal with as we seek what we want in life. They may in fact pose very real initial obstacles. But most of the time your limitations need not keep you from your goals.

For many years, I worked in a counseling center on New York's Lower East Side. Most of the clients I saw were trying to acquire more education or get into a training program where they could develop marketable skills. Among other things, we gave the clients a short aptitude test to help them decide what they might be able to do, or what they might need to develop to attain their objectives. At our very first session, one man told me that he wanted to go to college and study either psychology or social work—but he did not have a high-school diploma. He was self-supporting, black, and thirty years old. I gave him verbal and mathematics aptitude tests, and his scores were so low they did not register on the scoring scale— clearly indicating a severe limitation for somebody who wanted to go to college.

We discussed this problem and ways to deal with it, and he decided to work on his verbal skills. He knew he had to read, study words, and practice his writing skills if he was to be able to do college work. With this in mind, he read at least one book a week and wrote a log in which he recorded the main thoughts and themes of each book, citing the words that were especially troublesome to him. He then enrolled part-time in a college program and took a light load so that he could have enough time to complete the courses with satisfactory grades. He was thus able to deal with and decrease his limitations. To him the effort was worth it in order to get something he wanted very much—a college education.

Now, eight years later, this very same man has a high-school equivalency diploma, a four-year college degree, and is finishing his master's degree in social work. He was able to deal with what appeared to be almost impossible limitations without sacrificing his goals.

It takes effort if you want to "beat" your limitations. But the people who take the time to recognize and deal with them tend to find the effort more than worth it. In fact, a major task before taking action is to acknowledge your limitations so they will not surprise you along the way.

Many limitations, however, are more imagined than real

—imagined because people who have not taken action tend to devalue themselves. In a sense, they create more limitations for themselves than actually exist. For example, people who haven't worked for a long time often assume that nobody would want to hire them for a job. A housewife who has never been compensated for her very diverse skills as a homemaker thinks she has no "qualifications" simply because she hasn't been in a formal work situation; she complains, "I can't do anything." Likewise, many middle-aged people have told me that they know what they want but that it's impossible because of their age. For example, they think they cannot become lawyers or doctors because they are too old. While age may be a barrier to getting into a number of medical and law schools, it is not necessarily true that this limitation exists at all of them. Nor is law school the only route available to a person of any age who wishes to become a lawyer. For example, you can get law-school credit through correspondence courses or through certain work experiences as a nonprofessional working in a law office. I know of a woman who began her law studies at fifty-nine, and of another person who received a medical degree at sixty-five. Yes, age can be a real limitation in certain situations, but more often than not, its importance is overemphasized.

You may find yourself trapped by limitations unless you analyze them in relation to the given situation. For example, if you are one of twenty people applying for a job, the other nineteen may have your same limitations but may lack one of your assets that could more than compensate for your limitations. When you talk about a limitation, how sure are you that it is a limitation—and not just an easy excuse for copping out?

Now let's take stock for a moment. Pretend that you have your back to the future, that all you can do is look at what has already happened. As with most decision-makers, you are really only sure about what has happened.

Let's take the time to measure the assets and liabilities in your life to date. Look at your life broadly. Think about those special events, experiences, achievements, acquaintances, failures, and mistakes you can list as personal assets or liabilities. And don't forget your personal characteristics: the way you relate to people, the way you behave in various situations, and the way people tend to perceive you. To make this easier, I've provided a number of headings under which you can begin your inventory.

MY ASSETS AND LIABILITIES INVENTORY

Experience, Characteristics, Obligations, Needs	Asset or Liability	Possible Future Significance
Leisure activities and skills		
Example: Reading novels	Asset	Awareness of existing literature. Good word power and writing skills.
Special interests		
Paid work experience and skills		
Unpaid work and skills		
Volunteer activities		
Formal and informal education		
Family responsibilities and obligations		

Family resources _____

Personal
characteristics: _____

  Physical _____

  Social _____

  Psychological _____

The physical setting
in which I live _____

In what ways do your liabilities become obstacles to getting what you want in life? Are they real or imagined? If real, how do you know for sure? Now go back to your "possible occupations" list on page 51 and select from that list five or more things that you really want to do. Next to each, list those assets or liabilities that may help or hinder you in your quest to get what you want.

Things I Want to Do	Assets or Liabilities Related to Doing Them	Why I Am Sure These Assets or Liabilities Are Real
_____	_____	_____
_____	_____	_____
_____	_____	_____
_____	_____	_____
_____	_____	_____
_____	_____	_____

Finally, try to identify the major limitations that stand in your way. For each limitation, think of all the things you might do to reduce or eliminate it. For example, if a lack of work experience is a limitation, you might get into related volunteer work so you can cite some kind of work experience in applying for a future position. Or you might convert volunteer work into a paying business or job.

Major Limitations (Personal or Existing in the World Around Me)	Some Things I Can Do to Reduce or Eliminate Them
_____	_____
_____	_____
_____	_____
_____	_____
_____	_____
_____	_____

You may find it difficult or even impossible to reduce or eliminate all of the limitations. That is not unusual, so don't be discouraged. However, as a future reference, circle those limitations that you think are especially difficult. You may even be able to sidestep some of them without changing the limitations at all.

Take the case of Bob, who didn't perform well on aptitude tests. Because of this limitation, he could not get into the college of his choice, which meant a great deal to him. Since he was a good student, Bob felt he could do the most challenging work even though his test scores suggested otherwise. He investigated other colleges that had placed students as transfers in the college he wanted to attend. He enrolled in one of these, performed well in his studies, and was able to transfer to his chosen college after a year and a half. But this was not the end of the story. Later, Bob wished to go on to law school. Once again the entrance test proved an obstacle. And once again he chose another path. This time Bob managed to gain admission as a result of his excellent graduate work in another field.

Bob was not willing to settle for less than what he wanted in life in spite of real limitations. Alternative action and a little extra effort on his part were required, and there was no guarantee that Bob would get what he wanted in the end. His case is a good example of a person having to revise not his goals but the path to reaching those goals, in order to deal effectively with a limitation.

There are other limitations that you will become familiar with in the following pages. They include: not knowing what you want, not knowing how to develop alternatives, not being willing to make enough effort, not being aware of the real risks involved in a given action. These limitations, which hinder your decision-making skills, are the most crippling of all.

Chance

Often when I try to get people started on the difficult task of predicting the outcomes of decisions they are about to make, I am greeted with comments like "What's the use? So much of life is luck anyway."

True, there are many elements of chance, or luck, in life. But I want to identify two points that are especially relevant to the decision-making process. The first is the kind of chance that is associated with the circumstances in which you were born: for example, the degree of your family's affluence (or poverty), your physical and mental abilities (or disabilities), the geographical setting in which you live. Being born black and/or female—again a matter of accident—can often be a real disadvantage in many areas of our society today.

Such circumstances, the result of chance, should also be viewed in the decision-making process as either limitations or resources. They are part of your decision setting, aspects of your situation that you can be certain about and that you must face squarely in making a well-considered choice.

The other kind of chance that is of interest to us here is something that comes your way with minimal effort on your part. It's the luck you have when you win the lottery, sell a piece of land at a huge profit because a new highway is being built on it—or are stricken with a debilitating disease. In a sense, chance of this type injects an unexpected limitation or asset into your life.

Most "good luck" is in fact the result of some kind of action on the part of the "lucky" individual. Even winning the lottery requires your prior action in purchasing a ticket. The people who talk the most about someone else's luck are apt to be those who have not taken any action themselves. It might be said that after the hard work, the striving toward perfection, the dedication, the willingness to take action, all that is left over is luck. And sheer chance—the possibility of something wonderful dropping into your lap—is about as rare as stepping out of your house and being struck by lightning! If you sit and wait for that something wonderful to happen, you've probably let yourself be defeated before you begin.

Two major problems arise from the "I'll wait until it drops into my lap" approach. First, as I have said, there is a very good chance that nothing will drop in your lap— you simply won't be extraordinarily lucky. Second, if you are, and something does drop into your lap, you probably won't be prepared to deal effectively with your luck.

Some of the best and most tragic examples of this point can be found in the recent studies of people who won the jackpot in the New York State Lottery. While these people enthusiastically welcomed their initial luck at winning a million dollars, the outcomes were often disastrous. In case after case, devastation followed their lucky break. Broken homes, physical illness, severe mental problems, shattered family relationships, and a host of other problems seemed to erupt after these people were "blessed" with great wealth.

While you and I would probably like to take our chances and have a little of this kind of good fortune come our way, we should also know how to deal with it. We have to be prepared to cope with the aftermath of the achievement of a goal—whether we reach it through careful planning and action or by pure chance. Life doesn't stop when you're lucky, just as it doesn't stop when you experience adversity. And the irony of the stories of the sweepstakes winners is that their inability to deal with luck apparently forced them to suffer unexpected adversity.

Imagine for a moment that you have won the lottery. A million dollars! As soon as the word gets out, you begin getting calls from all kinds of people trying to sell you homes, cars, clothes, appliances, jewelry. On top of that, many callers will offer you very "good" deals involving discounts, possible high-yield investments, and so forth. You also begin to hear from a variety of charities, colleges, science-research groups, political organizations, and religious groups. Not to mention your long-lost relatives. Everybody wants your money. Overnight you have hundreds of decisions to make.

Assume that the money is tax-free (this is a hypothetical case). What will you do with it and how will you decide? Suppose you can only put $100,000 in the bank, so you have $900,000 to dispose of in other ways. Some sample allocations might be: a piece of land in the country, $50,000; a new car, $7,000; gems, $100,000; donation to cancer care and other charities, $10,000; college alumni fund, $10,000; season opera subscription, $300; cash gifts to children, $100,000; investments, $100,000.

With the above examples in mind, make up your own list.

Possible Uses for a $900,000 Windfall   **Amount**

After you have done this, you might share your list with your friends or your family to get even more ideas.

What did you observe as you made out this list? What does your list, the items and the proportion of your money allocated to each item, tell you about your values and the priorities of those values? Did you formulate a goal statement regarding what you want in life before starting this list? If you didn't, you may be headed for some regrets.

Revise your list in any way you want after rethinking it in terms of these questions, and then do one more thing. Try to predict some of the *outcomes* of your purchases, donations, or investments. Try to go beyond your immediate expectations. Make your predictions cover at least the next five years, and think of the bad as well as the good that might result from each of your actions.

Revised List: Purchases, Donations, Investments	Amount	Possible Outcomes, Immediate and Future, Good and Bad

One more task is in order. As you consider the outcomes you have predicted, ask yourself how certain you are about each one. Think about what information you would need to reduce the unknown factors involved in each outcome.

I hope it has now become clear that to make the best of even extraordinary luck you have to go through a total decision-making process. Your luck becomes simply the decision setting, or given, on which you must base your subsequent decisions. Luck does not excuse you from thinking through your alternatives, or from predicting the outcomes involved in them. To neglect the decision-making process is to be unprepared to manage the rest of your life effectively.

Social and Personal Pressures

Early in your decision-making, it is critical to begin to sense the subtle and sometimes not so subtle pressures that tend to move you in a certain direction. These pressures most often come from your peers and from the people important in your life. But they also come from things that you've learned which are so ingrained in your thought processes that you accept them as truths not subject to continuous reexamination.

You may be imbued with what is known as the "work ethic," so that you believe strongly in the value of working at your job whether it is a job that makes you happy or not. So you stay with that job because you *know* that that's what any self-respecting person is supposed to do. Another pressure comes from growing up in a society where success means everything. The more preoccupied you become with winning prestige and wealth, the less apt you are to explore options that may be more satisfying to you but that do not promise success as others have defined it for you. This pressure may confine you to doing what you have learned you *should* do instead of what you *want* to do. Against your wishes, you may feel pressured into emulating the behavior of the majority and feel fearful of not doing what others expect you to do.

As you get involved in the serious and difficult task of

making your own decisions, you must become sensitive to these pressures, be aware of their origin, and understand how they affect your judgment. You will need to predict what it might mean if you *do* go along with the pressures, and how that will affect your next decision. (Can you really give in "just one last time" and be free to go your own way in the future?) You will also need to predict the costs involved if you make a decision that goes against the grain.

While ultimately only you are responsible for the decisions you make, many of them will have some impact on others. It is important for you to be prepared for what the impact might be. You may have to ask yourself some difficult questions. How much do the others involved know about the realities of your decision situation? Is their future really affected by the decision you're making—or only their opinion of you? How will their happiness or unhappiness with the outcome of your decision affect you? How much importance are you willing to attach to their needs and desires? What would be the cost—to them and to you—of ignoring their wishes? Are you willing to pay it? There is no magical formula that can give you the answers.

Howard's case is a good example of conflicting pressures. He held a good job in a company that was relocating. Most people at his level were planning to move near the new headquarters, although the new location was not so far away as to make commuting impossible. Howard's family felt strongly about the ties they had established over the past five years in their community. His wife was a leading fund-raiser for several local volunteer groups. His daughter, entering her senior year of high school, was very upset at the idea of changing schools and leaving all her friends just before graduation. His son bombarded him with arguments about why they "just *couldn't*" leave. Howard himself loved their home and had put much of his spare time into improving it. He also treasured the many friendships and associations he had made in the community. At the same time, he was sensitive to the subtle pressure on employees at the officer level to move into the new corporate community setting. On the basis of his own and his family's feelings, he resisted pressures to move, and undertook the long commute to the new location instead.

Just six months after making this decision, Howard was informed that his department was being reorganized—without him. He also learned that some higher-ups in the company resented his not moving to the company "community," feeling that he could not be as effective a "team member" living at his distance. Out of work and with two children nearing college, Howard wondered about the price he and his family would have to pay for the decision they shared. Perhaps he shouldn't have listened to them. It was small comfort that they had shared in his crucial decision and were now obviously on his side during a difficult time.

As it turned out, Howard was out of work for several months, but because this period of job search also required him to look more critically at himself and his priorities, it proved well worth it. In his words: "I had become lazy in terms of constantly assessing what was important to me in my personal life and in my career. When forced to take a hard look, I really found that my family was important to me and I was more determined than ever to accommodate their wishes and mine. Ultimately, I ended up in a smaller company doing what I wanted to do. I still have a long drive to work, but to me this is a small price to pay for living in a setting where all of us are very happy."

Time Pressure

The final element to be considered in the decision setting is time. How much time can you allow yourself to spend on a given decision? How does the time limitation affect the number of alternatives you can develop and the amount of information you can explore?

Time is often a key to identifying a truly critical choice. When you feel you want more time to decide, it usually indicates that you are dealing with something important to you. This pressure will often cause people to back away from taking action and, consequently, from taking advantage of an opportunity. While time may help you to develop more alternatives and to study them more fully, it can also work against you. As time passes, options disappear or become irrelevant to your needs and wants.

Many people go through life searching for just one more alternative or piece of information. This can go on so long that when they finally find and use that better alternative, they are less well off than they might have been with an earlier option. Thus it is imperative to set deadlines for yourself and to make the best use of the time allotted. True, you may sometimes feel you have leaped before thoroughly looking, but this is perfectly natural. The main thing is that you have taken action to move in the desired direction. By waiting too long you may find yourself unable to move at all.

The element of time combined with the impact of pressure created a difficult decision situation for Suzanne, who became an unwed mother during her second year in college. Disappointed, hurt, and somewhat bitter that her boyfriend of two years, who was the father of her child, would not assume any responsibility in the situation, Suzanne was left to her own resources. She had to decide whether or not to give up her child, and she knew that this decision must be made within a few days after the baby's birth. In effect, she had very little time in which to make up her mind, since she did not fully realize the actual implications of giving up her child until after the birth.

In addition, Suzanne was being strongly urged by her family to give up the child. She had no real source of support for other alternatives, and she felt she was being forced to decide at a point when she was not prepared to make a well-considered, well-informed choice. Exasperated with what appeared to be a hopeless situation, Suzanne gave up her child. She regretted her decision almost immediately, as it became increasingly clear that she could have chosen other viable options. Now, five years later, Suzanne rates this period as a low point in her life. She continues to seek the whereabouts of her child, and she has focused her career efforts on counseling young unwed mothers so that they will be better able to deal with the pressures that she had to face in her critical choice.

In most cases, critical decision situations do not suddenly present themselves without warning of any kind. Too often, instead of preparing for something we suspect might occur, we wait for things to take care of themselves. We are then thrust into a more difficult situation than is necessary. How many people do you know who have ignored the warning signals of a failing marriage, a job in danger, a child in trouble? Or have even put off dealing with positive prospects, like what to do after college graduation? In general, you can deal from a position of strength with a far better chance of desirable results if you repeatedly examine what you want and begin to explore additional ways of getting it. When you do this, the time pressure becomes more a self-imposed deadline, one that you are more likely to meet because you're sure about who you are, what you want, and how you're moving toward it.

Your Critical Decision

All of the above elements in the decision setting will have some impact on your critical decision. Identify your critical choice again and try to assess it in terms of changes relating to yourself and the world around you that might affect your choice:

Areas of uncertainty in the setting that relate to your choice:

Limitations that you should be aware of:

Social and personal pressures acting upon your decision:

Time pressures that you need to consider:

6.

You and Your Values

I'm more and more realizing that I lived 50
years of my life without ever really coming
to grips with the very basic question of what
is and is not important to me, what is and
is not valuable and worthwhile. . . . I've
begun a process that my own kids began
almost from the beginning . . . developing
my own sense of values. I'm a beginner.
    —John Ehrlichman, *New York*
    magazine, May 10, 1976

The most important element in your world full of choices
is you. Regardless of your circumstances, the decisions you
face, or the life you want, your uniqueness makes the
choices in your life and even the setting for them special.
You may share with others similar circumstances, similar
goals, and even similar priorities in a given situation. But
only you and the things that represent you are brought
to *your* decision. The best decision for you may be very
different from the best decision for someone else. Likewise,
the result of your choice can only be fully evaluated by you.

This is a difficult point for some people to accept and
remember. It is often easier to follow or imitate others.
But given the freedom of decision-making, you actually
have the opportunity to break away from this "force field"
of imitation.

If you can begin to find out who you are, and in doing
so become aware of your individuality, you will be well on
your way to making well-considered choices that will yield

satisfying results. But if you fail to realize your own uniqueness, you will be bound forever to a life of doing what others think you should do.

The agony of finding out who you are is felt by all who really attempt this difficult task. Perhaps the feeling can be best summed up by drawing on the statement of a client who had come to an impasse in her life: "How can I be myself," she asked, "when I don't know who I am or what I stand for? I don't know what I want and I have no idea regarding what purpose I have or should have in life. Every time I do something, I wonder if it's me or simply my response to what I think others expect of me." The search to find out who you really are and what you value always has a cost associated with it, because you'll have to take some action in order to begin to respond to these questions. But taking action is the best way to grow, and observing the mistakes and successes in your actions will help you learn more about yourself.

Take the case of Ron Cooper. Ron, an educational consultant with a Ph.D. in psychology, decided to give up his lucrative practice and move to a rural town in New England where he opened a small gift shop. Over the years, Ron had realized that something was missing in his life. In the fast-paced world of consulting, he had little time to relax and give himself to anything or anybody other than his practice. He felt he would prefer a slower-paced life in a setting removed from the hustle of the suburban and city experience he had known all his life. His parents and friends were shocked that a person with his credentials would make this kind of move, and applied real pressure to dissuade him. But Ron's wife and children supported him and actually liked the idea of living year-round in this town, which they knew because they had spent vacations there. Ron is not yet able to articulate exactly what he wants. But he does think that the move will help him discover things about himself that will give him more certainty about the kind of life style and occupational pursuits that would be most appropriate for him and his family in the future.

Tricia also took action to find out what she wanted from life. Recently promoted to office manager in a large firm, she was getting close to the point where she could join the officer ranks of the corporation. While she was more than satisfied about her progress in business, she realized that she was getting further and further away from her old plan to perform with and eventually manage a small jazz band. What bothered her was that she was beginning to have doubts about what she really wanted to do. As she looked ahead, she saw that very soon she would simply lose the opportunity to do what was important to her. In order to test her own priorities, she decided to quit her job and devote full time to her music. She felt she had to act in order to find out if she was being truthful with herself.

This is not to say that you can't search while maintaining your present position. But these examples do show that the obstacles to finding out who you are need not appear too forbidding, too risky. How many times have you looked at your life and wondered if there might not be something more appropriate for you? And how many times have you rejected this thought because you believed you already had what others would be more than satisfied with? The hurdles of public opinion—and of the things you have been taught to believe are good for you—seem so intimidating at times that you don't even get close enough to take a look before you decide not to buck them. Ron and Tricia were struck by how good they felt when they attempted the leap. They knew they might not make it, but at least by trying they were giving themselves a chance.

This is the crucial point to remember as you study your

uniqueness: You may have to live in a crowd, but you do not have to imitate that crowd. It's not as difficult as it sounds. Already you are doing things that especially represent you in many different ways. The initial task is to sort out those things that truly represent you, those things that warrant some commitment of your resources. You may never find an absolute answer for yourself. But even if you later choose to do what the crowd does, you'll be doing it on your terms.

One way to begin your search is by taking a few self-inventories. First, write down three words that best describe you as a person. That's right—a three-word description of yourself. For example, I might use aggressive, effective, and restless to describe myself. What are the three words most descriptive of you?

1. _____   2. _____   3. _____

Don't be surprised if you find it difficult to come up with those three words. After all, how much time do you really spend thinking about who you are?

Next put down some of the things that you think make you different from at least some other people you know. These things might include qualities—for example, being considerate of others—or they might include hobbies, special skills, or the kinds of feelings you have or express. Write down as many things as you wish.

Personal Characteristics	Achievements	Special Interests
Examples: Gregarious, hard-working	I learned to play tennis	Japanese cooking, watching baseball games
1. _____	1. _____	1. _____
2. _____	2. _____	2. _____
3. _____	3. _____	3. _____

Now try to think of three words that you would like others to use when they describe you. Remember, this is the way you would *like* others to think of you!

1. _____   2. _____   3. _____

Finally, examine carefully these last three descriptive words. Do they reflect the uniqueness that you described in the first two exercises? Are they things that you are proud of? Most important, what kinds of feedback have you sought to learn if others see you as you would like them to? If you have trouble with any of these questions, chances are that you are going to have to do more searching for your uniqueness in order to show yourself in the way you prefer.

You will realize your potential as you independently choose with greater frequency and confidence the paths you want to take in life and as you use your freedom to express your own ideas. And you will become increasingly less dependent on others, which will lead to even greater personal freedom and a better chance to develop as a person. Thus you'll be adding new and unforeseen dimensions to your life. As a college student recently remarked in a decision-making class I conducted, "If everyone could make sound decisions, the various prisons in which human beings house themselves would cease to exist."

You Are What You Do

If I asked you to write down the things that are important to you in life, the things you cherish, the things you like to possess, and the things you like to do, you could probably come up with a long list fairly quickly. In such a list you would be making a statement about the things you value, and you would also be saying something about the standards of desirability that you apply to your life—standards that cause you to behave in certain ways and to do certain things. Every decision that you make should be based on some relevant value or principle, and to comprehend fully who you are and what you do, you must understand your values.

These values are learned, acquired, and developed, and they are subject to change. To be able to recognize and clarify your values, you must examine them continually— how you feel about them, what you say to yourself and others about them, and, most important, what you *do* about them. Most people do not take the time to examine their values. They assume that they have certain values that are automatically reflected in their decisions. Nothing could be further from the truth! If you do not subject your values to constant scrutiny, either by yourself or through discussion with others, you tend to make choices without really knowing what is important to you. Yet your values are involved in each and every aspect of the decision-making process.

Values affect the goals you set for yourself, the information you collect in studying your options, and the risks you're willing to take. While values are abstract in nature, they can manifest themselves in very concrete ways. Given the uncertain environment in which you live and the incredible number of decisions you can make in your life, it is important not only to understand what your values are, but to know how you acquired and developed them and how they influence your actions.

Value formation begins early in life. By the time boys and girls reach the third grade, for example, they can usually distinguish with great accuracy the values they hold regarding work. One can even observe at this early point a number of value distinctions based on sex. A long time before they got to the third grade, these youngsters began to acquire a sense of how boys and girls are supposed to behave. It is apparently clear to them that they're supposed to behave differently—at least in terms of those values related to future occupations.

Because values are learned and because they play such an important role in the decision-making process, it is useful to think about your values and where they came from. To make your task easier, I have listed a number of important values (see page 76), but you will probably want to add to the list other values that are meaningful to you. Designate the source from which you learned these values by putting a check mark ($\vee$) in the appropriate column.

Has this exercise helped you to discover new values you weren't aware of or new sources for your values? Circle those values that you've developed in the past five years. With new experiences and relationships, your values are likely to continue to change. In turn, this will have an impact on your choices and how you evaluate them.

Three levels of value development exist in each decision situation:

1. *Acceptance.* At this level you are willing to say that certain values, such as family, honesty, and prestige, are important enough to you not to reject them. In any given situation these values will have some impact on your goals, alternatives, and acceptable risks. But just accepting a value is normally not enough to help you make a well-considered decision.

2. *Preference.* At this level you begin to determine what values are most important to you in light of the decision you face. For instance, you might feel that you value job satisfaction more than prestige. Or honesty might have a lower priority on your scale of values when it comes to figuring out your income-tax deductions! Even at this level, simply being able to set priorities on your values

WHERE DID YOU LEARN YOUR VALUES?

Value	Parents	Close Friend	School	Religious Education	Spouse	Various Life Experiences	Other Sources
Honesty							
Family responsibility							
Comfort							
Opinion of others							
Friendship							
Prestige							
Excellence							
Competition							
Privacy							
Others:							

does not really mean that you actually value what you say you do. The missing component is commitment.

3. *Commitment.* This level requires that you act on your stated values. When you make a decision and then take action, your behavior represents a commitment to something you value. If honesty has a high value priority for you, you will file an accurate tax return even though you could list certain deductions that don't need to be substantiated. In this very simple example, you have forfeited money because you were willing to act on your value of honesty. This final phase of value development becomes a crucial factor in the choices you make.

To explore more fully the first two levels of valuing—acceptance and preference—consider the qualities and activities listed below. Obviously this is just a partial list, so feel free to add others. Once you have done this, put an "A" next to those values you accept and an "NA" next to those you do not. To determine your preferences, grade each value A, B, or C in terms of how important it is to you. Then place a "1" by your most important value, "2" by your second most important, and so on, until you have rated each one as A1, B3, or whatever. As you begin to recognize those values you accept and to attach some priority to them, you're on the way to unscrambling your values.

Choose the Values You Accept and Rate Their Importance to You:

Personal appearance	Prestige	Health	Others:
	Freedom	Equality	_____
Honesty	Orderliness	Money	_____
Winning	Possessions	Creativity	_____
Education	Power	Privacy	_____
Family responsibility	Learning	Love	_____

Now let's see if you can get some indication of what values you have actually committed yourself to. Suppose an anthropologist has decided to study you and your way of life. He is not satisfied by what you tell him about yourself and your values. He wants hard evidence and asks you for the following things:

Bills or canceled checks for the last five years
Descriptions of trips you have taken
Your favorite restaurant menu
A transcript of your formal education
Your contributions to charity over the past five years
A list of favorite TV programs
A list of your friends and their occupations
A photo album
Ten of your favorite tapes or records
Your most recent tax return
A list of groups you belong to
A list of things you no longer use but have not thrown away
The best gift you ever bought yourself

Consider what each of these items might tell the anthropologist about what you value. Each represents commitment on your part, and should be most revealing about what is really important to you. Look again at your unscrambled values. Have they shown up on the list for the anthropologist? Perhaps you'll want to alter or add to your list of scrambled values at this point.

Now I'm going to ask you to make an investment in your values. Starting with $100, invest from $1 to $100 in each value listed below. (You're free to add to the list.) The one stipulation is that you cannot invest the same amount of money in more than one value. Consider thoroughly before investing. Remember, you're starting from scratch. You do not possess any of the listed values until you buy them.

Values for Investment   **Amount You'll Invest ($1–$100)**

Ability to influence others
Physical condition
Chance for adventure
Intellectual ability
Satisfying sex life
Artistic talent
Income of over $50,000 per year
Attractive appearance
Job satisfaction
Happy family life
Travel
Mechanical ability
Social skills
Mental health
Prestige
Others:

_____	_____
_____	_____
_____	_____
_____	_____
_____	_____

Which values turned out to be most highly prized to you? This exercise should tell you a lot about your value priorities.

Value Conflict and the Agony of Choice

Ranking your values is no easy task. To complicate matters, you will constantly have to deal with changing priorities in each new decision situation. And you will probably run up against real conflicts in your value priorities. Decision-making then becomes an agonizing process that only a thorough investigation of self and available alternatives can resolve.

Jim's situation is a case in point. A hard-working executive, with a family to whom he is very devoted, Jim jealously guards his time so he can spend his weekends with his children. He also values their future and wishes to provide for it adequately. Suddenly he is promoted to a highly responsible position in recognition of the fine work he has done for his firm. It is clear that this job will require working many weekends away from home. He wants to accept it because it will make the future of his family financially secure. On the other hand, it will mean giving up much of his leisure time with his children. If he refuses the offer, he may never have another as good.

If you were Jim, what conflict would you be feeling? How might you deal with it in order to make your choice? What is the best "bright" future for one's children? Is there any way Jim can accommodate all of his values in this situation?

Jim's values could not all be accommodated in his current situation. But by examining the conflict involved, he realized how important his job success was to him. He simply could not give up his goal of reaching the top at this point in his life, and he realized that at least for the present this would take a certain degree of priority over spending time with his family.

Similar value conflicts turn up at all levels of decision-making. I did a study of the decision-making carried out by eight presidents of major United States corporations in 1975. As I began to interview these people, I was curious about their awareness of their values and how those values affected their decisions. Predictably, a high priority for all these presidents was to provide a quality product at a competitive price to the consumer, with an acceptable margin of profit to the corporation. This involves three values—quality, price, and profit—and each is related to the other two.

I introduced each president to a hypothetical situation containing a value conflict. Suppose, I said, they learned that their plants were having a severely adverse impact on the environment in terms of air or water pollution and that this was affecting a large number of local residents.

For most of these presidents, this was not so hypothetical, for they had actually been faced with similar dilemmas. One company invested great sums of money to correct the situation, and as a result its ability to remain competitive in price was affected. Another company decided to take action only if all of its competitors did. Still another company decided to do nothing until the government or some other authority told it exactly what to do. For each company caught in this conflict, a different kind of action was taken based on the president's value priorities, influenced by corporate value priorities.

Each president accepted the value of protecting the environment. Yet each expressed a different preference, and only one made a commitment to the value. It is very much the same in your personal decision-making. Simply saying that you value something is not meaningful until you ask: relative to what?

In a community where I used to live there was a very active organization dedicated to equality of opportunity and civil rights. This group undertook projects and gave money to support these concerns. However, when the group was presented with a local situation involving the exclusion of certain children from participation in a number of social functions apparently because of their ethnic backgrounds, the organization opted not to take action because some of their children were members of the elite groups attending the functions. Relative to their children's happiness or the positions these people held in the community, their espoused cause was apparently not important enough to them to get them to pursue action.

Conflict will arise in virtually every decision you make. Only the rare one-value person escapes conflict. Most of us have many values that have to be ranked every time we choose. The one-value person does not have this problem. Some people have money as their only value, others have power, and still others have winning.

At first glance this appears to make life relatively simple. It doesn't. The ramifications of the one-value approach are far from appealing. In fact, a one-value person becomes a kind of automaton. If his one value is winning, this robot will do anything and everything to win, whether or not it's legal or moral. Today there is evidence in every field, from athletics to politics, supporting the notion that there are a lot of one-value people around. Most of them ultimately do suffer the consequences of their lack of concern for others. While you might be able to proceed as a one-value person in a limited sphere, sooner or later actions dictated by a single value will come into conflict with the larger, more complex value systems of other individuals and groups.

Let's take another look at your values from the acceptance to the commitment level. First, take an inventory and list the ten material possessions you value most. Ask yourself why they appear on the list. What do you value about them? Your list can include large or small things—a house, a car, a stereo, a favorite photo, a piece of jewelry, a book. They need not be your possessions with the highest monetary worth, simply those you value highly for one reason or another.

**Ten Material Possessions I
Value Most**   **Why I Value Each**

_____   _____

_____   _____

_____   _____

_____   _____

_____   _____

_____   _____

_____   _____

_____   _____

_____   _____

_____   _____

Now imagine that, owing to a variety of circumstances, you can keep only three of these possessions. Which three would you choose and why?

Three Material Possessions I Prefer Over All Others

Values That Influenced My Choice

_____   _____

_____   _____

_____   _____

As you narrowed your choice from ten to three, what did you have to consider? What conflicts did you encounter in making each choice? You might begin by considering what you had to give up in order to keep the three.

Material Possessions Retained

Value Conflicts Encountered

_____   _____

_____   _____

_____   _____

Material Possessions Given Up

_____

_____

_____

Did your decisions cause you to think beyond your own personal world? Did you find yourself considering others close to you, or the values of the world around you?

Of course, it is one thing to make hypothetical lists. It is quite another to take action when you are actually faced with a value conflict in a real-life situation.

At this point, go back to your list of unscrambled values and preferences. Try to recall a real action you have taken that shows some commitment to those things you say you value highly.

Values That Have High Priority for Me	A Recent Action I've Taken to Show This Value Has a High Priority
Example: Family	Sacrificed fishing trip to take children to Disney World.
_____	_____
_____	_____
_____	_____
_____	_____

When you get to the commitment point, you're really coming closer to finding out who you are. Let's look at this from one more perspective. Think back over the past week and try to remember what you actually did during each day. Think of everything—the tasks you enjoyed and those you didn't, including work and leisure activities. Your record should reflect the specific things you did and the amount of time you spent doing them. What you especially want to observe is whether or not you're doing what is really important to you.

Now let's take a closer look at the way you're spending your time. How much is spent doing what you'd prefer not to do, and how much doing things important to you? Do you find that you do the most enjoyable things more or less than the others? Note that an activity that shows up on the list as enjoyable is not necessarily more important than things that were listed as not enjoyable. Activities you don't enjoy may be important to you for other reasons. For example, you may not like to cook, but you might spend a lot of time doing it because your family enjoys your meals. In this case, your preferred value is making other people happy. Or you may be holding a job you dislike because it enables you to travel or maintain a special hobby. What I'm getting at is that any action you take, whether it is enjoyable or unenjoyable, tells you something about your values.

MY ACTION LOG

	What I Enjoyed Doing	Time Spent in Hours	What I Didn't Enjoy Doing	Time Spent in Hours
Monday				
Tuesday				
Wednesday				
Thursday				
Friday				
Saturday				
Sunday				

Mainstream pressures, discussed in chapter 5, converge on nearly every choice we make. There is a current cry for honest politicians, for instance, but many people believe it is impossible to reconcile honesty with politics. Similarly, how principled can a businessman be? How candid can one be in any activity, whether it be education, sports, medicine, law, public service, or science? The answer is clear: You can be as honest, as principled, and as open as you want to be in any walk of life. However, somewhere along the way you will experience conflict. Regardless of the choice and the values represented by it, there will be a cost involved. If you're honest, you may not be able to attain high office. If you are too principled, you may not advance rapidly in business. If you're too open in any endeavor, you may find doors closing or ears being plugged because of your candor. But the choice is yours. Ultimately you are what you do!

Now, thinking back as far as you can, recall at least two decisions or actions that have had a significant impact on your life. List each one below. Then try to decide what each action or decision represents in terms of a statement of values. What did you value in each of the actions? Did the actions reflect your values, or the values of people close to you—or even the values that you felt existed in the social context in which you acted? What was the main reason or value underlying each decision? Try to recall the conflict of values in each choice, the struggle of going from acceptance of the value involved to outright commitment to it.

Values Reflected in the Major Actions of My Life

Major Decision	Value(s) Involved	Value Conflicts Experienced
_____	_____	_____
_____	_____	_____

Your Critical Decision

Now apply the same process to your current critical decision:

Values Involved	Value Conflicts Experienced	Priority Values for Any Action Chosen

Your quest to find out who you are and to determine what you're willing to commit to your goal in life has just begun. I hope you are discovering what is important to you and just how important these things are, since any well-considered decision hinges on your awareness of your values and their order of preference in a given situation.

Goal-Setting

One of the biggest stumbling blocks in the decision-making process is the movement from exploring and clarifying your values to a clear statement of your goals in life. A young man who has completed graduate school asks, "How can I be sure that this is what I want?" A woman whose children are now in college observes, "I don't like what I see in store for me the rest of my life. But what can I do when I don't know what I want?" And a man facing retirement is concerned because he doesn't know how to move toward what he has vaguely called enjoyment. In other words, without something specific to reach for, you are apt to suffer a kind of paralysis in life. You feel that you're standing still while time flies by. And opportunities disappear with time. This stagnation is frustrating because you sense that you are missing your chance for self-fulfillment.

A great deal has been written about pursuing goals. Knowing something about where you want to get and what you want to become is important because direction will provide a focus for your energy, resources, and time. Getting a goal statement together is a way to get started because it forces you to move from the general to the specific. If, for example, your goal statement is to attain a comfortable and happy life, you will immediately have to identify specific qualities that you consider essential for such a life. Often, because we are living in a goal-oriented society, we are rushed into a commitment before it is even clear to us what goal we really want to pursue for ourselves. Young people are constantly asked, "What do you want to be when you grow up?" And their answer is usually one that is geared to the questioner's expectations rather than a true reflection of what the young person really believes. The kind of answer usually expected is the naming of a specific profession, such as doctor, engineer, or computer programmer. But it is actually much more useful to consider the whole constellation of values in a goal statement before trying to deal with the specifics. This leaves the door open for consideration of various avenues for achieving the values that are important to you.

Thus, in answer to the question above, rather than doctor, an appropriate response might be, "I want to help people but also maintain some chance to really express myself. I like hard work but I expect to be rewarded or recognized for it in some way, and not just through a good salary." Naturally, the person responding this way has a lot of clarifying to do, but this initial statement forces one to look at what is important and why as more specific goal statements are developed.

The other day, I shared some goal-setting activities with a middle-aged man. After a number of exercises, he observed that it was really easy to decide what to do but he could not get up enough commitment to do it. I suggested that *this* was the time to take a closer look at what he valued and how much he valued it!

Values are the guiding factors in establishing your goals. They provide the personal involvement in what you envision as successful goal attainment. The main task in goal-setting—as in the entire decision-making process—is to reduce the unknown to the point where you are clear regarding what you want. And then you must decide how much it is worth to you to go after this goal.

The starting point is to define what you know about yourself, your values, and the world about you, and to use this knowledge to determine a direction. You have already begun the process by examining your values and the commitment you have to those values. However, this kind of searching, observing, talking, and discovering does not mean action. You should act only after your search has been translated into a clear goal statement.

Recently, in one of my decision-making classes for mid-career adults, I asked the group to specify a goal by thinking about what they wanted. Some of their responses were:

"To know and use my talents to the fullest advantage."
"To get out of debt and achieve security in the future."
"To improve my relationship with my sons."
"To establish a meaningful relationship with a person of the opposite sex."

All of these statements indicate that growth of some kind is a priority. But they are too vague to be clear goal statements.

Your statement of intention must be clear enough to allow you to formulate necessary actions to reach your goal in a reasonable amount of time. For example, suppose you have taken a careful inventory of what is important to you in a job. You conclude that helping others is what you most desire. Your goal then is to find some kind of work that embodies this high value priority. Think of all the jobs that might involve helping others, not just those that you might like to do.

You probably came up with jobs like teacher, insurance salesman, social worker, lawyer, psychologist, traffic guard. Obviously such a list could be almost endless. It is now also obvious that the goal statement is not clear enough to help you fasten upon a specific occupation. What caused this problem? For one thing, you have to define what you mean by helping others. The whole list of your value priorities must be brought to bear here. You may want a job that helps others, but perhaps not if it requires you to do something illegal or immoral, or if it doesn't have a certain degree of status attached to it. So what you need to do at the beginning is to determine the values related to your goal and to arrange them in order of priority.

Dream a little and pretend you have been offered the chance to spend the next 365 days anywhere you wish. Your general goal statement might be to find a place anywhere in the world, in which you can spend an ideal year. In this case, you are especially fortunate because you do not have to worry about the cost involved. Everything will be paid for. All you have to do is choose the place. As you begin your search, develop a list of possibilities. What are some of the things that would make your year ideal?

Things to Make an Ideal Year _____

_____

_____

Things That Would Constitute an Ideal Place _____

_____

_____

After you have studied your lists, rank your priorities from most to least important.

Then consider each of your lists and complete the following statements:

An ideal year for me means _____

_____

An ideal place for me requires _____

_____

You may find that the statements are rather lengthy, but that's all right since you're just beginning to clarify what you want your ideal year to be. In the process, you are beginning to translate what is important to you into a form that will help you set some specific goals. You may already have thought of several practical alternatives that could move you closer to your ideal year. At any rate, you have taken two important steps toward successful goal-setting. First, you have consciously articulated your values. Second, you have made a personal, albeit general, statement about what you want to achieve. In short, you have begun to design your life.

Turn now to some goals you have actually been thinking of recently. They may be family-oriented, occupational, financial, social, cultural, mental, spiritual, or physical. In the space provided below, write a clear goal statement for each of these areas as they relate specifically to your life. (If an area is irrelevant to you at present, simply leave it blank.) Here are a few guidelines to consider:

1. Be clear about your value priorities. Ask yourself, "What will this goal give me that I value?"

2. Be sure your goal statement is clear enough to identify specific actions that can be taken to attain it. A statement such as "I want to lose weight" will not necessarily help you come up with a plan of action. Weight

problems may relate to physical conditioning, to diet, or to your glands. Each cause for being overweight might require a different kind of action. A clearer statement might be "I want to improve my physical condition so that I can run a mile three times a week in less than eight minutes." This goal might, in fact, cause you to lose weight or to redistribute your weight so that the shape of your body is more appealing to you and to others.

3. Establish some time limit or target date. This not only helps you get under way, it also gives you an opportunity to check your progress along the way.

4. Initially, select a goal statement that is manageable, one that does not depend on an unseen future event in order to bring it about. If your goal is to achieve a certain style of living, it should be one you can achieve without winning the lottery.

CURRENT GOALS

	Goal Statement	Values Attained	Time Limits or Progress Checkpoints	Possible Actions
Occupational				
Financial				
Family				
Social				
Cultural				
Mental				
Spiritual				
Physical				
Other:				

You can see how important and difficult it is to be specific about your goals. Writing them down is generally helpful because it forces you to examine them more closely.

Obstacles to Goal Attainment

Once you are able to establish clear goal statements, your next task is to predict what obstacles you might encounter, and to develop ways of dealing with them. Some frequent obstacles include:

Obstacles relating to self: lack of confidence, motivation, or time; fear of change, of making a mistake, of failing.

Obstacles relating to others: being sidetracked by family responsibility; yielding to peer pressure; yielding to pressure from relatives; lack of encouragement from people close to you; backing down in the face of resistance from others.

Obstacles relating to the decision setting: having an unusual or new kind of goal quest; having values and/or goals that conflict with societal values and/or goals; deviating from societal expectations; having to find more "acceptable" or obvious courses of action; being limited by your environment in some way.

Once you have begun to identify obstacles, you should, in a very preliminary way, seek ways of overcoming those obstacles. This might mean developing new actions for reaching your goals, or a revision of your goals along the way. To return to the general statement "I want to lose weight," any number of actions might be taken to achieve this goal. Some obstacles are: lack of will to eat less; lack of time available to exercise; change in your priorities along the way. For example, the outcomes you expect from losing weight might be to look and feel better, which may be important to you now but could become less important if you find that the effort to lose weight is putting you in a bad mood or affecting your relationships in a negative way. Consequently, you may wish to revise your goal, or pursue a different path to reach your goal.

In offering guidelines for formulating a clear goal statement, I suggested that the goal statement should be under your control, that it be one you can manage without a lot of outside help or unforeseen good fortune. You will encounter fewer obstacles if you begin slowly and carefully. Take a few small assured steps as you begin to move toward what you want. For example, if your goal is to make a new friend this month, the first small step might be to join a group or club. This small action may get you to your goal as quickly and as effectively as relying on a more ambitious approach, such as giving a party for new people in your community. Lots of things can go wrong with a party, which in turn could be destructive in terms of goal attainment.

One of my clients offered a good example of how even a tiny step can really get you moving. Ethel, a middle-aged woman with grown children, wanted to go back to college and complete her degree. She had been out of school for a long time, and she was very anxious about what she might encounter on her return to an educational setting. For years Ethel had not taken any action because the obstacles seemed too great. She confided that she thought the professors would laugh at her and that she feared she could not compete with other students who were more familiar with the demands of academia. But she learned that she could enroll in a course that did not require any papers or exams, a course designed to help people who were considering a return to college. In this nonthreatening environment, Ethel found that she could indeed deal with the educational setting. She has now embarked on a degree program as a full-time student. The first small step, a kind of tryout experience, helped remove many of the obstacles, real or imagined, that were preventing her from realizing her goals. Now she is formulating additional goals—like what kind of work she wants to do after graduation.

As you begin to move toward your goals, it is especially

important to be aware of self-sabotage efforts. The weight watcher who has decided to jog finds there is not enough time for it in his schedule. A teacher who vows to improve the writing skills of her students finds she has little time to correct papers properly because she has volunteered her time to a number of other school projects. The parent who has promised to spend weekend time with her children takes on additional weekend work at the office.

Other people can sabotage your movement toward your goal as well. If you're a woman, your career goals may be halted if you listen to relatives who tell you that you'd really be much happier in your marriage if you raised a family first. If you decide to return to school and leave your children with a sitter, you can count on the fact that critics will be looking closely at your children for any abnormal behavior. Recently, a woman friend of mine ran for the state legislature. Several people we talked to later claimed they did not vote for her because they were afraid of what might happen to the children if she was elected!

Another factor that can impede goal attainment is the impact your behavior has on others. You might ask yourself, "What will other people notice about me as I move toward my goal?" This can actually be both a positive and a negative factor: negative in the sense that you'll want to be sure to anticipate any negative impact on others that might lead to attempts to hinder your efforts; positive because it is a good check on whether or not you're progressing toward your goal. For example, people will make observations about your schedule, how you look, and so forth. This is helpful because it will tell you that you are moving and developing in ways that others are noticing.

To develop practice in dealing with sabotage and the impact of your behavior on others, try the goal attainment inventory on page 96.

GOAL ATTAINMENT INVENTORY

Goal Statement:

(Make a clear
goal statement)

Potential Self-Sabotage	Possible Attempted Sabotage by Others	Impact of Your Behavior on Others When You Take This Action	Things to Anticipate When Goal Is Attained

Actions I Can Take to Reach This Goal

1.

2.

3.

4.

5.

One more potential problem in goal-setting is the misunderstanding that once you achieve a goal, it will provide you with some kind of absolute satisfaction in your life. While it is undoubtedly satisfying to attain a goal, you will rarely be satisfied indefinitely with your attainment. Rather, you must be prepared to handle the question What do I do next?

Earlier, I mentioned a woman who had begun her pursuit of a law degree at the age of fifty-nine. She went on to complete her degree in three years. At that time I asked her what she was going to do now that she was a lawyer. She thought for a moment and then replied, "I don't know for sure, but one thing I do know is that I'm going to cause some trouble!" While this woman attained a very important goal, she now had to decide what she wanted to do with the rest of her life. She was not content to frame her diploma and simply look at the goal she had worked so hard to attain. Any one goal is only a step in a certain direction.

If you have worked long and hard to achieve a particular goal, the experience of no longer having it to shape your life can be particularly disorienting. We have all heard stories of people who "fall apart" after reaching the success they have striven for over a number of years. Many women have described the consequences of having only one life goal: to be a wife and mother. Once their children are grown, they find themselves with twenty or thirty blank years ahead of them. Or what of the person who has finally become president of the corporation—and is still dissatisfied?

One of the most poignant expressions of this dilemma came from an ex-convict. This man had spent thirty-nine of his forty years in institutions—many of them prisons, as well as orphanages and foster homes. His goal was to be free, but when he was finally released and was outside the prison walls he said, "I look out and I don't see those towers with the guards and I guess I should feel good. But I've left the known for the unknown and that scares the hell out of me." Freedom had been his goal. But what should he do now that he had attained it?

Your Critical Decision

As you think about your critical decision, you should begin to ask what results you expect from the choice that you are about to make. Try to ascertain what additional freedom you will be achieving for yourself when you reach your goal. How can you build on these new opportunities? How can you use your expanded life space to move toward new and more satisfying options?

My Goal Statement Related to This Decision Is:

Values Related to My Goal	Actions or Steps I Can Take to Reach My Goal	Target Date	Outcomes Expected
_____	_____	_____	_____
_____	_____	_____	_____
	Obstacles I Might Encounter	**How I Might Deal with Obstacles**	
	_____	_____	
	_____	_____	
	What I Might Do to Sabotage My Efforts	**What Others Will Observe About Me as I Move Toward My Goal**	
	_____	_____	
	_____	_____	
	Some Other Goals I Might Pursue in the Future as the Result of Attaining This Goal	**My Progress to Date: Specific Actions Taken**	
	_____	_____	
	_____	_____	

7.

Finding the Best Alternative for You

It's not what you don't know what gets you into trouble; it's what you know for sure that ain't so.

—Mark Twain

David's long-range goal was to deal actively with urban problems, perhaps through city government. To this end, he began law school after completing his master's degree in history and education through a two-year program in the teacher corps. Six months later, he decided to drop out—a very painful decision for him. He had no trouble doing the work, but he found that his studies involved memorizing legal precedents without digging into the underlying causes.

David decided that he would have a better chance of reaching his goal through his undergraduate studies in urban planning, rather than by working toward a law degree. While today he is still unsure of the best path for pursuing a career in urban planning, he has begun to build an approximation of his own best path. Currently, David is teaching in an urban setting and has become actively involved in community organization projects.

This young man's experience is a good example of what is involved in choosing a course of action to reach a goal. Usually there are many alternatives available. For example, if you wish to complete a four-year college degree, one obvious way is to enroll in a four-year college program. However, given your unique circumstances, your preferences, and your resources, this might not be the best or even a possible alternative for you. Consequently, you might choose to work and go to school part time. Or you might be qualified to take examinations and get college credit for your performance on those examinations. You might also have some of your work or life experiences evaluated for college credit. You could join the military service and earn credits while in the service. You might even take a two-year college program and complete the third and fourth years as a part-time student or through correspondence courses. These and other alternatives are viable ways to complete a four-year degree program. Your task remains: to explore the advantages and disadvantages of each and choose the best alternative for you.

Try to recall a critical decision that you made in the past. What were the alternatives available to you? What action did you take? Why? If you have trouble recalling a decision, think about the following:

Choosing what to do after high school
Your first job choice
Selecting a place to live
How you chose your spouse
Your decision to have a family
Your choice of a new car

If you were to make the same decisions today, would you have other alternatives? Would you seek more or different information before making your decision?

Two limitations in selecting an alternative should be kept in mind from the beginning: you will probably never be aware of all the alternatives; and you will usually not be able to experience the alternatives before choosing. These limitations are two of the major reasons people avoid making choices. In the first case, people are reluctant to decide until they have examined all of the possibilities. But because we live in a changing world, many alternatives may be just around the corner, and others currently available may disappear. The same problems arise if you attempt to try all of the alternatives before choosing. In addition, each trial has some cost attached in terms of time, energy, money, and other resources. You must decide before you've looked as much as you'd probably like to look, and you must make a commitment without experiencing the alternatives.

A good starting point is to develop a wide range of alternatives for yourself without initially rating them as acceptable or unacceptable. (This will come later when you start to collect, evaluate, and utilize information regarding your choice.) Unless you do this, it may appear that there are only a few and sometimes no available alternatives. Through your unique set of life experiences, and your incomplete knowledge of things, you might tend to eliminate many realistic courses of action. Thus your field of alternatives is prematurely reduced, severely limiting your chances of coming up with the best one for you. An important decision-making skill, then, is to expand the number of alternatives that you actually consider before making a choice.

To do this, you have to rid yourself of a lot of preconceived notions about what is suitable or unsuitable. Try making two lists when you are faced with a decision. On one list put all the alternatives that you would now pursue or consider pursuing as a way to reach your goal, regardless of how unrealistic or fantastic they may seem. On the other list put all the things that you feel you definitely would not pursue. Write them down as quickly as they come to you, and don't worry about whether they seem "far-out" or impractical. After all, you're not committing yourself to anything at this stage. To give you a sample decision to focus on, go back to the exercise on page 51 where you were told that you could no longer do the work you were doing at the time. I'm going to add one more element to this situation: You are in a state of desperation. You have been out of a job for months, and badly need work. It might help to write down a few of the things that being desperate means to you. Is it being totally without financial resources? Is it having nobody in the world to ask for help? Or is it being in a state of depression and despondency? Desperation might cause you to jump at the first available possibility as a quick or easy way out. Or it might force you to become far more imaginative than you would be under ordinary circumstances.

Now, while you are feeling really desperate, consider what you would do given the fact that you can no longer perform your present work. Think, dream, fantasize, and create all of the alternatives that you could pursue. Write them down in the two columns below, making the list as long as you can.

Acceptable Alternatives   **Unacceptable Alternatives**

_____   _____

_____   _____

_____   _____

_____   _____

_____   _____

_____   _____

If you have the opportunity, you might garner even more ideas by trying this exercise with your friends or members of your family. What you are doing is building a list of possibilities—appealing and unappealing, realistic and far-fetched—that you *could* pursue before refining the list.

Go over each list and put a check mark next to each alternative that meets two or more of the following criteria: (1) You have *valid, factual* information that has led you to find this alternative acceptable or unacceptable. (2) The information comes from an expert of some sort, and there is no emotion involved in his judgment; it's a matter of objective data. (3) The information has been reexamined by you recently enough so that it is still relevant. (4) Your information is inadequate but you have a strong feeling or at least some sense that this is either a poor or a promising alternative for you.

If you are like most people, you will find many items in each column that you are not able to check because you lack sufficient information. Reexamine your list. Eliminate from both lists all the alternatives that you are now sure are unsuitable. How much closer are you to choosing the best one? What additional things do you want to know before you can reduce the list even further? Write them down.

Think about these things. Designate at least one source under each of the following categories:

People You'd Like to Talk To:
(Are there experts or authorities that you should be in touch with?)

Things You Want to Consider About Yourself:
(Have you clarified your values and priorities enough?)

Things You'd Like to Read or Research:
(Do you know what printed information is available and where you might get it?)

Places or Agencies You'd Like to Visit:
(Are there special places set up to help people like you?)

Experience That Would Prove Helpful:
(What things have you done that can provide useful information?)

Other Opinions That You'd Like to Have to Corroborate Those You Already Have:
(If you believe something is true, can someone corroborate it?)

Emotions That Might Affect Your Choice of Alternatives:
(Do these emotions relate to experiences, or to things you have learned in the past?)

This is a rather long but important procedure to give you the feeling of the kind of searching necessary first to expand your list of alternatives, and then to pare it down.

Your Critical Decision

Now try to make a similar alternatives list for your critical decision. Remember to ask yourself whether you feel under heavy pressure or even desperate to make this decision. What influence is this having on your development of alternatives?

Acceptable Alternatives   **Unacceptable Alternatives**

Apply to this critical list the information criteria described above. Where can you start looking for more and better information?

Seeking Information About Alternatives

You can become even more sensitive to your information needs by selecting the one alternative that you would pick if you had to make the choice this instant.

What was the main reason you chose it? What additional information would help convince you that this is the best choice? How certain are you about the outcomes of this course? Might some of the unacceptable alternatives turn out to be acceptable if you had more information about them?

The key to choosing your best alternative is the information you collect, evaluate, and utilize. This information is not always easy to come by, nor is it always easy to evaluate. Here are a number of guidelines to keep in mind whenever you seek information:

1. *Even "experts" have limitations as information sources.* When you do locate a promising source of information, be sure to ascertain what self-interests, emotions, and ulterior motives that source might have. Can the source offer valid, relevant, complete, and objective information? Probably not. Even so-called information "experts," such as stockbrokers, lawyers, doctors, and travel agents, have limitations that need to be realized. A travel agent is obviously a good source for travel information, but he might also have a special package that he's pushing that month. Given the same set of circumstances and information, one cancer surgeon might recommend a radical mastectomy, while another might consider chemotherapy a more effective treatment. In addition to checking some additional sources even when experts are involved, it is especially important to know what questions to ask in your information search. After all, it is *your* decision and, consequently, *your* resources that will be committed to any action that is taken. Selecting the good information from the bad is a major element in effective

decision-making. Regardless of how reliable you think a source might be, it is useful to ask him three basic questions: Why are you suggesting this? What makes you certain that this is the best option? What other alternatives are there?

2. *The order in which information is collected may affect the decision you make.* Not only are sources important, but so is the order in which information is received. The influence of the first source you employ may cause you to gather information that would be quite different if you had gone to another source first.

Consider the case of a woman who wishes to return to college to study economics. Before she consults her family, she explores various colleges, talks to admissions people, and finds out the cost and the kind of time she will need to give her studies. She then discusses her plans with her family. Another woman with a similar goal decides to consult her family first. The first woman will have all the information together before talking with her family—and thus she will be able to respond to the family's questions with greater confidence. The second woman may find herself overwhelmed by her family's questions and decide that returning to college will be too difficult. On the other hand, she may receive useful suggestions from her family that will facilitate her later search for information. Both situations could have advantages and disadvantages. And in both cases the order in which sources are consulted might well affect the final decision.

3. *In the initial stages, you need to keep your options as broad as possible.* Far too often, people tend to lay out alternatives for you. As a result, you may focus on only those alternatives. But you should always keep in mind that there may be other alternatives that haven't been mentioned by anyone. Also, you are bringing what is uniquely you to the situation, so that an alternative that may be best for most people may not be best for you.

4. *Information about alternatives should include information about outcomes.* If you find yourself in a desperate situation, you may choose something for the sake of immediate survival without considering the consequences. However, the outcome may prevent you from pursuing other things that would be more suitable over the long term. In thinking of outcomes resulting from a course of action, there are two factors to consider: (1) How probable is it that the result I want will occur? (2) How desirable is the result? The best alternative for you will represent some weighing of how probable something is against how desirable it is. (More on this in the next chapter.)

5. *Before you collect information, it is vital to have a clear sense of what you want.* A goal statement is essential on two counts: first, it gives you some direction regarding what information to look for; second, it requires you to generate at least a preliminary statement of what is important to you in the situation. Without knowing this, it is impossible to judge how desirable the outcomes of your choice will be, which in turn inhibits your ability to choose your best alternative. Thus, as you can begin to see, the process of decision-making eventually comes full circle. The beginning is a statement of your values to clarify what you want. The circle is completed when you decide what alternative you are willing to commit yourself to based on its desirability—determined by the knowledge of how important something is to you.

Bill's goal was to complete a master's program in social work. After obtaining his B.A. in sociology, he applied to the graduate school he wanted to attend, which offered the program at a tuition he could afford. At the same time, Bill enrolled in some graduate courses as a nonaffiliated student, a perfectly acceptable practice. Bill received a response saying that while his qualifications were excellent, there was simply not enough room in the program, and he had been assigned to the waiting list. Nothing opened up, so Bill reapplied for the following fall semester and continued to take courses as a nonaffiliated student. He received high grades in all his courses. In the spring he again received word that although he was well qualified for admission, there was no room for him, and he was again assigned to the waiting list.

At this point, Bill saw himself getting no closer to his goal. He could take no more credits as a nonaffiliated student that would be transferable if and when he was admitted as a full-time graduate student. He sought out the dean of the graduate school for advice and was told that he had two alternatives: he could apply for admission again the following fall, or he could apply to another graduate school nearby.

Bill decided that neither of these alternatives was suitable in terms of getting him closer to what he wanted. He needed to develop another alternative, and he decided on a very unusual one: to pursue the alternative he had been told was not available.

He took the second letter he had received to the admissions office and asked, "If I am qualified, why am I being put on the waiting list while others are being admitted? What is the distinction that is keeping me out?" The answer was far from satisfactory, so he took his questions to the dean of graduate studies. Here he also received unsatisfactory answers, but he did get a promise from the dean to investigate. To make a long story short, Bill went through virtually the entire administration of the university before he received the final word that he was accepted as a full-time student.

Bill effectively pursued two important requisites to find the best course of action. First, he increased his alternatives —and thus his freedom of choice—and his method of doing this was somewhat unusual in that he pursued a supposedly unavailable one. This in itself is a good lesson, because we often eliminate alternatives based on incomplete or inaccurate information. Second, Bill's persistence in his quest enabled him to check out the accuracy or validity of the information he received. By doing so he was able to keep the alternative he wanted alive. Essentially he asked: "How certain are you that this alternative is not possible for me?" This forced the university to come up with the facts.

Bill had to struggle to get what he wanted. He was able to make that commitment because he was very clear regarding his goal and what he thought was the most desirable way to reach that goal. Had he been turned down, Bill still had other alternatives. If he had opted to reapply, he might have received more careful consideration. In addition, along the way he learned about how to deal with the kind of impersonal, inaccessible bureaucratic institution that many people face in seeking to attain their goals.

Making Use of the Information

Because good information is crucial to finding the best alternative, it is important to be alert to a number of factors that can either hinder or help you in making the best use of that information.

Listening: One of the most important skills in decision-making is knowing how to listen. Listening should not be thought of as passive. It is something you should prepare yourself for if the information you seek is important in terms of the decision you are trying to make.

Keep these three questions in mind: (1) What information do I need, including new information I might look for? (2) Am I really clear about the information I've heard? (3) How can I be sure that I have heard what I think I've heard?

The first question involves some preparation on your part. The second requires that you ask for clarification. And the third can be answered by using a tape recorder, taking and checking notes, discussing what was said with somebody else present, or reading an unbiased account written by somebody else. Naturally, you should also evaluate the content according to the guidelines previously discussed.

Keeping an Open Mind: It is not uncommon to begin a search for alternatives with certain preconceived notions. This may be all right as long as your attitudes don't prevent you from looking at other alternatives. You must learn to pay attention to all kinds of information, even the kinds that irritate you or that you think are not worth considering. In other words, try to take an objective look at everything before rejecting anything. Recently, a young woman told me that one reason she chose a college in the Midwest was that her father had told her Eastern girls were snobbish and unappealing. It is possible that this father could document his statement from his own experience—but it is also true that, armed with such a negative generalization, he is unlikely to see or acknowledge any contradictory evidence that comes his way. The result of such prejudice is that the decision-maker misses out on much valuable information and many worthwhile alternatives. It is impossible for anyone to begin to learn what he thinks he already knows.

During the 1976 Presidential campaign, a series of TV commercials very effectively built on what might be called the public's "mind sets." They showed a variety of "real people" telling why they were for or against a candidate. In one ad, a person above a sign reading "Atlanta, Georgia" would say, "I'm from Atlanta, and I'm for

President Ford because I never saw Jimmy Carter do anything good for Atlanta." The viewer had no idea who the speaker was, how accurate his judgment might be, or even whether he was giving his honest opinion. In short, the speaker was a poor source of information. The commercials were effective not because they gave out helpful information but because they tended to reinforce what some viewers already thought about a given candidate. This can be a classic mistake—accepting information simply because it reinforces what you already have in mind.

A good way to check your listening skills (and a good demonstration of the danger of seeing and hearing only what you are predisposed to) is to listen to a speech by a politician whose policies you dislike. Write down the five most important things that he or she said. Then compare your responses with a friend who feels differently about this politician. Or you might be interested to see how two newspapers with opposing viewpoints covered the speech.

Overvaluing Experience: Experience comes cloaked in a variety of forms. All too often we find ourselves accepting something that was dictated by another person's experience. A mental warning bell should sound when you hear someone say, "Listen, I have much more experience than you in these matters."

There is nothing inherently wrong here—a person with a good deal of experience in a number of similar situations wants to share what he has learned with you. But when the decision involves you personally, another person's experience should be treated as only one kind of information and no more. Remember that experience is tailored to the individual person. It is rare that another person brings exactly the same values, goals, and priorities to a situation that you do. For one thing, the other person's experience may be out-of-date. For example, a mother, drawing on her own experience of more than thirty years ago, counsels her daughter regarding whether or not to raise a family. But even if the other person's experience is current, it may not apply to you in many ways, because you are bringing your own variables to the situation.

Even your own experience should be considered as suspect. Sometimes if you have a success in one situation you may try to repeat that experience in all situations. For instance, you decide to invest in a condominium in Florida because you have spent your vacations there for years and have always enjoyed it. But there are lots of attractive investments in warm-weather climates suitable for retirement that you have not experienced. Before you choose, some information beyond your personal experience should go into your decision if you want to optimize your chances for selecting the most satisfactory alternative.

On the other hand, a bad experience can turn you away from trying something again. In spite of the inconvenience it causes you, you refuse to use a certain airline because when you took a previous trip the attendants on that airline were rude. Or your first camping trip was a disaster because of bugs, cold food, and bad weather, and consequently you have never gone camping again. But it's important for you to realize that everything is subject to change, and your experience might be different at a different time in your life. Moreover, an initial bad experience does not necessarily mean that something can't be done to make the next one more successful. As Mark Twain said, "We should be careful to get out of an experience only the wisdom that is in it and stop there; lest we be like the cat that sits down on a hot stove lid. She will never sit down on a hot stove lid again—and that is well; but she will also not sit down on a cold one any more."

Another pitfall associated with experience is the tendency not to try something new and unfamiliar. Think back to the exercise in which you chose an ideal place to spend a year. Were you trapped there by this experience pitfall? We often tend to make the safe choice, to pick something that we are sure of because of our previous experience. Thus, if a person has spent many vacations in Florida, he might later decide to retire there even though other places might offer more appropriate settings for the kind of retirement life he's seeking. Experience can lull us into the selection of the familiar, whether it's the best alternative or not.

On the other hand, as I mentioned earlier, the quest for experience can greatly retard our decision-making process. Some people want to experience all of the alternatives before they settle on one. I actually heard a college professor tell his class that the *only* way to decide whether or not to have children was to experience having one!

Experience, then, is of limited usefulness when you are reaching out for your future. Don't be afraid to leave it behind.

Knowing Something for Sure: Do not fall into the trap of unreservedly accepting any statement that begins with: "I know for a fact that," "I'm certain the following will happen," or "We've studied all the data and we've concluded that," etc. Most acceptance occurs when you get these words from "an authority." Often it happens because you agree with the rest of what the person says, or because you *want* to agree with it.

Without carrying it to the point of overkill, always try to check yourself when you're feeling certain about something you know or that somebody has told you. More often than not, you will be better off recognizing that you do not know something and admitting it. What really leads to trouble is knowing something for sure, only to have it turn out not to be so. Think of the number of times we have heard "I am sure" or "We are certain" about public issues such as the Vietnam War, the energy crisis, or alleged

corrupt activities of men in government and business—
statements that later proved not certain at all. Or think of
the investors who have lost their shirts putting all their
money into a "sure thing." Learn to be especially alert
when someone is certain, or when *you* feel certain about
something.

In the next section, I'll discuss probabilities and ways to
become less uncertain about your choices and their results.
But rarely will I be able to cite an example of something
I am absolutely certain about. I hope that you will come
to appreciate the difference between being absolutely
certain of a result and being certain of the likelihood of
something happening. It's an important consideration in
moving toward the outcomes you want.

Holding Out for More Complete Information: As we
come to the final elements in the decision-making process,
I want to describe one more stumbling block to taking
action: the search for complete information. When you
make a decision, you try to collect information that will
enable you to reduce the unknowns involved in your
choice. You will rarely, however, get all the information
you want nailed down in an objective, accurate, and
complete manner. You will almost always have to decide
without all of the information you'd like to have in hand.
If you don't accept this, you will find yourself forever
collecting information and never making a choice. Time
is working against the decider in this situation, and I can
give you no magic formula for knowing when you have
enough information. You are the one to decide on that
point, based on your ability to be certain enough about
the results that are the most important to you. So be
prepared to take action before you feel you have looked
enough. It might make you a bit uncomfortable, but it will
get you moving, whereas the search for complete information is apt to lead to no decision at all—or at least to the

disappearance of some very promising alternatives. As René Dubos notes in *Man Adapting*, "Decisions must often be taken before all facts are in hand. Effectiveness of action must never be sacrificed at the altar of complete intellectual understanding."

Emotion and the Decision You Make

Up to now, I have talked mostly about the objective elements in the decision-making process, but many critical choices involve a large degree of subjectivity. You may examine all of the facts about a group of job applicants and then choose a person who does not measure up on paper because you have a good feeling about him or her. For most people, the choice of a spouse is primarily emotional; their inner feelings make the difference. But the appallingly low success rate in marriage, regardless of how success is defined, would appear to make a good case for the shortcomings involved in decisions based primarily on emotions.

The fact is that it's "only human" to expect our emotions to be part of our decision-making process. The trick is to begin to recognize and control the role emotions and feelings play in your decisions. There are two kinds of emotions that you should be aware of in making a choice. They can be described as "uninformed" and "informed" emotions.

Uninformed emotion is the one you try to eliminate from your decision-making process. To cite a classic example of the power of uninformed emotion, in the infamous Salem, Massachusetts, witch hunts in the late 1600s, with no evidence presented against them, dozens of people were put to death—not because they were caught in the act of casting spells, but because they would not admit their guilt, or because they maintained that it was wrong to punish people solely on the basis of unsubstantiated accusations. A similar kind of mass hysteria occurred almost three hundred years later, during the Senate inquiries into Communism in the government. If you did not support Senator Joseph McCarthy's point of view, you were apt to be considered by many to be a Communist. Uninformed emotion can rear its ugly head quite often in the decision-making process, and the person deciding this way is likely to pay the consequences.

Informed emotion is quite another thing. It stems from a real commitment based on fact—that is, you believe in something so much that you can easily make a commitment to it. Take the following case, where informed emotion played an important part in a decision made by a large corporation. This corporation had rigid objective requirements for launching new publications in terms of the number of years they were willing to finance them. If the profit profile was negative after a predetermined number of years, a product would be dropped. This time limit was held to steadfastly until a certain magazine was introduced in the early 1960s. The decision-makers believed strongly in this product; based on their knowledge of the market, they felt it had great potential. Yet, at the end of the three-year trial period, their publication had not made it. Nevertheless, with little more than feelings to go on, they ignored their own rules and continued to publish the magazine for six more years before it became profitable. The magazine was *Sports Illustrated*—the most profitable in its field today.

So if one believes or feels strongly enough about something, it can become a kind of fact. In some ways, it becomes even more powerful than fact. If belief is running very high and strong, contradictory information will not be accepted, because the individual doesn't believe something contrary can be true. This kind of behavior can play havoc with your life and with your decisions as well—but, as in the case above, such commitment can also carry the day when the objective signs are against you.

You will probably need to rely on your gut feelings in some of your decisions, and that is fine. Generally, when you have the feeling that a certain action is right, it means that you should be taking a closer look at what is really important to you. In other words, get as close as you can to recognizing *why* you feel that way.

Emotional facts become especially important in interpersonal relationships, a common and often painful area of decision-making for all of us. The following case illustrates what I mean.

When Donna came to me with what she described as a very critical decision—whether or not to renovate and redecorate her home—I was a bit puzzled about why a discussion like that would make her so tense and upset. I soon learned the reasons.

Two years previously, Donna had discovered that her husband, Tim, was an alcoholic. While this did not come as a complete surprise to her, the seriousness of the problem did. Her husband had begun to leave home for several days at a time. He would sometimes call to report what he was doing, but his periods of absence increased in length until at one time he was gone for several weeks and Donna received no word from him. Finally, in desperation, she called his office and learned that he had not been in for a week. But because his work was conducted on an independent schedule, his office was not concerned, and he had in fact left a number where he could be reached.

After trying this number for several days without getting an answer, she managed to locate the address. She found Tim in a completely helpless state, curled up in a corner in a rooming house. She called an ambulance and got him to a hospital, where he was brought back to health. She then phoned his office and talked to the president of the company, explaining that her husband was an alcoholic.

This company had a program for alcoholics, and they enrolled him with the warning that if he returned to his old ways after his cure they would fire him.

After taking the cure, Tim returned home and resumed his work on a regular basis. But fearful that he would revert to the bottle, Donna kept track of him constantly, as one watches to keep a small child out of mischief. By the time I talked to her, this period of crisis had lasted for two years. Donna no longer felt any love for her husband, and in fact she very much resented having to spend her time keeping him away from trouble. She wanted to get him out of the house and out of her life as soon as possible.

However, with two children in college she had no assets except for one—the house. While the house was valuable, it was run-down and in need of expensive repairs and redecorating. At present, with Tim working, she could begin to put the house in order and pay the college bills, but Donna was certain that as soon as she severed relations with her husband he would revert to alcoholism.

Donna decided to take care of Tim until she was able to complete the major repairs on the house and find work. Her most important goal was to begin to live the kind of life she wanted. The only way she felt she could do this was by achieving at least some degree of financial security and no longer having close contact with the husband she had come to despise.

Donna did have other alternatives. She could have found work immediately and let her husband try to survive on his own. She could have found some form of assistance, so that her husband could receive aid in another setting where she would not need to have daily contact with him. She could have tried to discover some workable arrangement whereby she and Tim could continue as husband and wife. She could have asked her children to pay for their own education, or at least a large share of it.

The action she took seemed to Donna to be the quickest way to attain her goals: a life of her own and the opportunity to work so that her children could complete college. Her alternative may seem cruel, and Donna herself admitted this. But she felt she had done as much as she could do, and that by hanging on, she would have no chance of happiness for herself. This decision was made in the context of suffering that can only be understood at first hand.

When she made her decision, Donna's emotions may have caused her to be less than thorough in evaluating what was important both to her and to those around her in this situation. In addition, she did little in terms of predicting the outcomes of her choice. She focused on the immediate situation, which for her was personal survival. To optimize the quality of her choice, she should have turned her attention soon to the future as well—and to the expected and unexpected results with which she would have to contend.

As an effective decision-maker, you will need to examine often what is fact and what is emotion in your choice. If you can be sure about the alternatives and the objective data you have used, the rest is informed or uninformed emotion. And as you become more skilled as a decision-maker, you'll have an easier time identifying what portion of your choice was based solely upon emotion. You can easily begin this process by looking at the last important decision you made. It should be a fairly recent one so that you can recall how you went about making it.

In one column below, list all of the objective information you used, reasons that you can support to some extent with evidence. In the other column, list those things you could not support by any hard evidence, things you felt or had some kind of hunch about.

The Decision: _____

Reasons Based on Evidence for Making the Decision I Did	Factors Based on Opinions, Educated Guesses, Emotions
_____	_____
_____	_____
_____	_____
_____	_____

In the second column, put an "I" next to the items that represent informed emotion and a "U" next to those you would rate as uninformed emotion. Just to make sure that emotion did not enter into any items in the first column, check each one by asking, "How and why am I certain that the item is true or accurate?"

Keep emotions in mind as we move to the real cutting edge of any choice—assessing the probability and desirability of the results of the alternative you choose. Both the emotions you might bring to a choice and the emotional content of the information you utilize are vitally important.

Putting It Together

This is an appropriate time to take a careful look at the decision-making model and to review where we are now in the process. You have already learned some new things and clarified other things about yourself. In addition, you have seen the relationship between values and goals, and between alternative-building and information-gathering. Now it's time to put these elements together.

If you turn briefly to the Model for Critical Decision-Making on page 23, you'll note that you are about to enter Phase V. Here you have to select from among the alternatives you have developed—not an easy task. If you have used and evaluated your information skillfully, the various alternatives often seem to have positive and negative aspects that initially defy making a single choice.

At this stage you assess all the things you know in order to predict the outcomes of each alternative on your narrowed-down list. But this transition from fairly solid data to the realm of prediction is difficult for most people. It requires that you be on solid ground in the decision-making process thus far.

Although you may have gathered information and assessed clearly what you want, all kinds of things work on you at this stage—including your emotions—so that once-appealing alternatives don't look much better than any of the others. Where is that compelling conviction you wish you felt?

This was exactly Al's case. Al had one of the most secure jobs around in a nonprofit educational organization. People never seemed to get fired, the organization had a bright fiscal future, and the benefit package for employees at all levels was so generous that a number of his co-workers referred to the company as "the Golden Casket." Most of them said they couldn't afford to leave such a secure situation. Al had worked hard and had outstanding evaluations during his ten years with the firm. He had never really thought much about the benefits until his eldest son and daughter began nearing college age, and the company's college tuition benefits looked more and more attractive.

Suddenly, a decision was made to phase out the program that Al directed, and he was offered an unappealing alternative program. Al had to work fast to develop alternatives, for in six months he would be in need of some other form of livelihood. Here's the way he reasoned, in his words.

"Just like that, I'm cut loose in six months. My reaction is a mixture of disbelief, sadness, anger, resentment, and a big lump in the stomach. What about the four kids, the travel plans, the things Meg and I have planned? Well, it's fish or cut bait now. What are my alternatives? Secondary-school teaching, guidance, university teaching, postdoctoral study, a lesser job in my present company, drive a cab, work with a foundation. None of these seem very appealing except for university teaching. Most clearly represent a step down. There must be something better.

"What are some of the things I've been dreaming about and wanting to do? Start my own consulting firm (the timing seems good for this); co-consult with a psychologist friend who has an office established; write for a living (what I've always wanted); teach at a university part time and consult. These alternatives look much better but they're all high risks. I may not be able to move into them so quickly or easily.

"And how would they maintain the goals that I feel are vital to my family at this point in our lives? Meg to finish college (one year left); son to start college next year; gymnastics training and college for daughter (gymnastics now, college in two years); travel; basic financial commitments—house, car, loan payments.

"Making this list, I realize that my family is of high value to me in anything I decide to do, and I also realize that I will fight like hell to maintain a style of living that will give us as a family a chance to learn, to grow, and to enjoy life. I don't want to cut back on our current life style even though it might be necessary in the near future. I need to plan for that eventuality.

"I also notice that I'm beginning to feel better. I'm thinking with a new kind of clarity. Perhaps the prospect of proving myself at forty is exciting and important to me. Well, here goes—do I have any guts? I've said my most important values were independence, creativity, and family, but do I really mean it? Oh, I've got a few things to back me up: two 1973 cars that I own; a house that the bank owns a lot of; a cabin in the country that I own; some summer income; potential book royalties; some consulting contacts; good health; and $4,000 in savings.

"Not a great picture, but not bad either. A lot of questions continue to run through my mind. What if I don't have something firm in six months? How will I react to Meg and the kids—will I be more irritable? How will I feel about myself—a failure, a washout? And how will others react to me? By trying to help—or avoiding me? (After all, they could find themselves in the same spot.) How will I feel if I make it? And how will the change in life style affect all of us and our friends? I can really see that I may have to alter my behavior somewhat. I may be more dependent on others and that means I'll have to extend myself to others more, something I have trouble doing at times.

"Yet, all in all, I feel this is a good thing. As a person I was getting lazy, careless, not thinking ahead, and really not taking stock of myself. Maybe that good income, with even more coming along in a routine way, had led me to lose control of my own life. Soon I'd have been fifty, and perhaps I would have just gone along that much more easily being dishonest with myself—after all, those benefits are impressive! Well, now the benefits are gone, along with the secure job and the future that needed no planning. But I feel O.K. It's a new life and a new growth opportunity and there is something good out there for me."

Al went on to develop his alternatives and decided to set up his own consulting firm so that he could take advantage of the contacts he had established. In terms of maintaining his security and current style of living, this was probably the highest-risk alternative on his list. But it does permit him to be independent and creative, to arrange his schedule so he can be with his family more often, and to move toward writing full time. In an informal way, Al made a synthesis that enabled him to look at what he knew and what he wanted and to plug them into his alternatives as he began to compare them.

Your Critical Decision

Drawing on the best information you have about yourself, your decision-setting, and your goals, describe how each alternative you have developed accommodates what you know and how it will get you closer to what you want.

Alternatives	What You Know Would Be Accommodated by This Alternative	Why It Would Get You Closer to What You Want	Is This Alternative Realistic for You? Why?
1.			
2.			
3.			
4.			
5.			

8.

Predicting and Weighing the Risks

Sooner or later everyone sits down to a
banquet of consequences.
—Robert Louis Stevenson

Just knowing about possible courses of action does not by
itself provide a sound basis for making a choice. Some
looking into the future is necessary. You get closer to
solid ground when you collect information about the
likelihood of something happening if you choose a certain
course of action. This helps you to identify the uncertainty
that may exist in a given action and to plan for dealing
with that uncertainty.

Begin looking to the future early in the decision-making
process. Make a list of the expected results of your alternatives, both positive and negative. For example, "If I do
go back to work, I will learn and grow as a person, but I
may also have to care for my family when I am physically
and mentally exhausted; this may cause other problems
for me that will have impact on my family and on my
work." Be sure to predict the possible results of the current
course of action you're pursuing, as well as any new
alternatives.

As you polish your skills you can begin to predict the
outcome of each available alternative in terms of its

probability and its desirability. Taking action almost always involves weighing what is likely to happen, and how worthwhile or desirable it is from your perspective. When you play the lottery, for instance, the odds may be a million to one against getting the outcome you desire. Yet thousands of people put down their fifty cents, dollar, or two dollars regularly, not because they have a good chance to win but because the possible outcome (perhaps as much as a million dollars) is so desirable that they're willing to risk the loss of a small investment.

When you bet on the lottery, at least the odds are clear and you know what the monetary return might be (the degree of desirability). When you gamble on a course of action, it is more difficult to determine how probable and desirable the outcome will be. Yet we must make choices. The result is that we often find ourselves acting on partial information, hunches, educated guesses, and only rarely on solid, objective information.

Circumstances are never exactly the same, even when you're facing the kind of problem you've solved before. Therefore each new situation calls for assessment of yourself and your present setting. Think back to a decision that you now believe was one of your worst. Imagine that you have to make that same decision today. How would you make it? What would be the difference now? In addition to reflecting on what you learned from the decision the first time, what new assessments would you make of yourself and the world around you before making this choice again?

One of My Worst Decisions	Things I Learned from That Decision
_____	_____
_____	_____
_____	_____

New Things I Would Have to Consider If I Made the Decision Again

_____

_____

_____

Unless you are quite unusual, you will find that there are many new elements facing you today even though the decision you're facing may seem almost identical to one you dealt with in the past. These new elements must be considered carefully if you are going to improve the course of your life. This may sound obvious, but it is much more difficult than you might imagine. At the center of the difficulty is the realization that few of your decisions are made under conditions of absolute certainty or truth. The span of any existing certainty or "definiteness" is subject to change as you deal with a new situation with its new options. The more you look, the more you will discover new facts that will alter the degree of uncertainty in your choice.

This uncertainty can be costly. When you commit your resources to a course of action, you will almost always have to give something up. This process is well illustrated in the television quiz shows, most of which operate in the same way. At an early point in the quiz, the participant can usually accept a rather modest prize or "go for broke." If he elects to go on, whatever he has won thus far must be given up—with no guarantee that he'll end up a grand-prize winner. As in game shows, if you choose to go for the jackpot, you have to be willing to risk some of your resources. People often decide on a certain action without thinking very much about the possibility or the desirability of the outcomes. For most critical decisions, this area of neglect—failure to assess outcomes—is the most common cause of unsatisfying and even devastating results.

Probability and Decision-Making

All potential events are either possible or impossible. The task of the individual in the decision-making process is to find out how probable or likely something is. When you say something is probable, you are saying that you know something about its chances of resulting from an action you take. Whenever you can attach a probability to the possible outcomes of a choice, you are talking about the degree of risk involved in a choice.

The word "probable" has many meanings. We say: "It will probably snow tonight." "A 90 percent foul shooter will probably make all his foul shots in many of his games." "The probability for getting 'heads' or 'tails' on a fair coin toss is fifty-fifty." "There will probably be a black President someday."

In each case, probability draws its meaning from the different types of knowledge upon which it is based. Probability may be based on a subjective guess, a rough estimate, or on some subconscious notion. You may also combine subjective and objective evidence in the form of an educated guess—for example, if someone is six feet four and weighs 230 pounds, you will probably assume he is stronger than most people who are of average height and weight. More concretely, there are certain traits and skills that can be measured and used to predict future performance. (One college uses a specific combination of high-school grades and SAT scores to predict freshman grade performance.) Finally, there are straight mathematical probabilities based on known factors, such as the chance of rolling a seven on the toss of the dice.

Try to think of probability as a matter of degree—that is, the result of your choice is less than a hundred percent sure and more than unknown. If you now hold a job, for instance, it is *possible* that you might become president of the company even if you see that as only a slim chance.

What you may not know or even have a good way of knowing is how *probable* it is that you'll become president. When you begin to collect information to answer the *"how* possible" questions, you are dealing with the probability involved in the situation. If, for example, you are the number-two person in the company, it may not be absolutely sure that you'll succeed to the presidency, but your chances are very much better than they would be if there were ten vice-presidents ahead of you.

In some cases, probability may actually be very measurable. In baseball, a manager decides to walk an opposing hitter because he has a high probability of hitting a home run. The manager has information about each batter, how many home runs he has hit against what kind of pitching and in what kind of game situation. This evidence tells him that it is less likely that the next batter will hit a home run. Note, however, that such a probability statement is based on a large number of observations in nearly identical situations. Your personal choices will rarely offer you the opportunity for so many repeated observations.

Beware, particularly, of assuming probability based on one observation. When a friend of yours tells you that the car he has is the best one he's ever had, it does not mean that this will most likely be the best car for you. Even setting aside the differences in a car, your friend's single experience is simply not enough to go on. He might have acquired one of the few exceptions in a long line of lemons.

Two types of probability emerge: the first takes on a purely objective view and says that you can only deal with probability if you're involved with events that can be repeated over and over again under identical conditions, a kind of laboratory experiment where variables are controlled. The second involves a more subjective or personal approach.

Personal decision-making will require that you deal as effectively and as efficiently as possible with the subjective approach to probability, although you should make every effort to get as close to objectivity as you can.

To get the feel for this, let's test your skill in attaching probabilities to possible outcomes. Look to the future and complete at least one of the columns across by responding to each item.

What Would Be the Outcome If You:	Possible Outcomes That Might Occur	Your Estimated Probability of Each Outcome	Probability Information Sources
Example: Quit your job today	Not get another job	10%	Bureau of Labor Statistics Talk with placement office Know people who quit in similar situations
Went back to school			
Decided to do what you really want and like to do			
Changed your residence to another part of the country			
Lost your job today			

Do your best to predict all of the outcomes, both good and bad, before you attach any probability to them. Once you have made your probability assessment, ascertain the source from which you derived that probability. If the probability was derived from at least two or more observations that you made under very similar circumstances, rate the source of the probability you assigned an "O" for objective. If it involved less than two observations under similar circumstances, mark it "P" for personal or subjective probability. Go one step further and try to respond to the question "Why am I inclined to give it the rating I did?" Was it due to a hunch, a feeling, or an educated guess? Or was it based on some evidence that you think is accurate and appropriate given the situation?

Remember, there are lots of vague probabilities bandied about that we tend to accept without relating them to our own situation. We assume, for example, that a graduate of a four-year college has a better chance of getting a job than does the high-school graduate. But, in fact, statistics show that in many states at least half the college graduates do not get the kind of work they want, and some get no work at all. Most high-school graduates may earn lower wages, but they do get jobs, and they have not invested four years of time and money in a college education. If you do decide to go to college, you cannot afford to neglect the probability that you *may not* find a job, or at least not the job you want. Otherwise you may be in for a harsh surprise.

In another area, it is true that few marriages are rated by the participants as successful. In fact, depending on the figures you read, about four of nine marriages, nationally, end in divorce, while eight out of ten are deemed less than satisfactory by the participants. So the probability of having a good marriage would appear to be rather low. But low compared to what? The other alternatives do not typically guarantee a high level of satisfaction either, so how do you make a choice? Do you avoid marriage because of its high probability of failure? Or do you marry and work toward the possibility—with the lower probability— that your own marriage will be a success?

As you reach any point in your life where you have

to choose an alternative, you will find two kinds of situations occurring. On the one hand, you will be faced with alternatives with known probabilities in terms of outcomes. Marriage and admission to college based on grades and test scores are two critical decision situations in which you can get fairly good information—at least as it relates to the general population. On the other hand, you will be in situations where the outcomes of your choice are relatively unknown, and where there isn't any data relating to the general population that will be of much help to you. When you wonder about the results of taking a job promotion or of returning to work after many years at home, when you adopt a child, or when you decide to retire, there is little in the way of known probabilities about how things might turn out for you. In fact, initially, the results of the action you are contemplating may appear as a huge and foreboding question mark—an unknown. As you begin to anticipate outcomes and collect information to clarify the likelihood of those outcomes, you develop the power to move from the unknown to the known, and this is where you truly begin to deal with the risk factors in your choice.

The Real Meaning of Risk

Compared to your current relatively safe and familiar existence, a new opportunity will often appear risky. Normally, this initial feeling is caused by the prospect of having to give up something you know to reach for something you're not sure you'll like, be satisfied with, or even attain. Consequently, risk is often perceived as something negative. It is interesting to me that even in Webster's Seventh New Collegiate Dictionary all the definitions of the word "risk" focus on the probability of loss, injury, or peril.

As we use it, risk is the *known probability* of what might

result if you decide to pursue a certain action. Consequently, it involves the chance for gain as well as for loss. The fact that you have a 50 percent probability of getting greater job satisfaction through a new job offer also implies that you have a 50 percent chance of dissatisfaction. Risk, then, means that some degree of positive payoff is coupled with the negative or low aspects of the situation. This alone means little until it is examined in light of the value you attach to something happening—that is, its *desirability*. Most of us are fairly safe risk takers in that we like to operate in the realm of at least a fifty-fifty chance. Yet millions of people play the lottery and get married, even though their chances for success with each are far less than fifty-fifty.

So, ultimately, you will have to assess the probability of an alternative's having good results in light of its worth to you and how it might compare in probability and worth to the other alternatives available. The idea, then, is not to eliminate risks but to take the right risk for you. In addition, whether the information is objective or subjective, different people will differ in the degree of their belief in that information even when they have virtually the identical evidence. For example, you and your friend listen to the weather report and are told there is a 75 percent chance of rain the next day. You may have less faith in the weather report than your friend. You go ahead with your plan for a picnic while your friend cancels his. Your personal belief in the probabilities for the same event differ.

As we have said, much of what you will be trying to predict in terms of the outcomes of your choices will not have clear probabilities. At best, you will be evaluating potential results based on such terminology as "a very good possibility," "a so-so chance," or "a very small chance." Because of the one-shot nature of most choices and because of the changing factors involved, you will have to build your own probabilities by getting the best information you can and coupling it with a real knowledge of what you want in life. Information will help you arrive at some personal probabilities regarding outcomes, and these probabilities will have to be considered in light of how desirable the outcomes are for you. When a person decides to run for an office in a local political race, that is exactly the kind of model he might follow.

Let's look at that situation for a moment. If you were to decide to run for local office, some of the outcomes might be:

The effort might take several years.
Much money would be required.
You might have to win the support of certain important and powerful people you don't like.
You'd have little family life while running.
You wouldn't be elected.
You would be elected.
When in power, you'd have more say in getting things the way you think they should be.
Many things you say would be published and publicized.
You might have much less private life while in office.

The list could go on ad infinitum. Each outcome would have a degree of probability and desirability attached to it. When a potential candidate assesses all of the outcomes in terms of probability and desirability, he or she will make a choice. If one candidate decides to run while another decides not to in the same race, it will most probably be based on a different personal weighing of each possible outcome in terms of probability and desirability. It is the desirability weighed with the likelihood (probability) of something happening that gives us a clear look at whether or not a certain action is worth the risk involved. As you will see, the worth for individuals involved even in the same choice will be quite different, because individuals *value differently* and consequently attach different degrees of desirability to a given outcome. Before I explore this notion further, let's take a look at your own risk-taking behavior.

Look back on your life for a moment and try to think of the biggest risk you've ever taken, particularly one that you felt to be a very high risk at the time. Write it down, along with the reasons you have for rating this a high risk for you.

My Greatest Risk   **Why It Was a Great Risk for Me**

_____ _____

_____ _____

_____ _____

What did you know for sure about the risk involved? What were the known probabilities associated with this risk at the time and how sure were you about these probabilities? Why were you willing to take this risk? Would you take the same kind of risk again? Why? Do you have more information now, and would it take on a different kind of importance for you at this time in your life? What kinds of information would you seek now that you did not know about or seek when you first took this risk?

As you go through this exercise, what may begin to unfold is a different perspective about how desirable the outcomes of this risk would be to you today, as opposed to sometime in the past. You are beginning to formulate a plan of action for a similar future decision with similar risks based on different values and different priorities. Many people have told me of their greatest risk and added that although it turned out to be worth it they would not take the same risk again. Some people say they are too old, and others say that attaining the goal would no longer be as urgent. The point they are making is an important one for you to keep in mind—that is, risk or the likelihood attached to an outcome is not significant until you study the desirability of the outcome as well.

Perhaps the whole weighing effort that goes on between probability and desirability can best be clarified through a case that was reported in the *New York Times* in March 1975. A twenty-year-old, nearly blind college student accepted a $165,000 out-of-court settlement of a malpractice suit minutes before a jury voted to award her $900,000. The suit stemmed from alleged malpractice at the time of birth resulting in blindness in one eye and near-blindness in the other. The young woman, who was studying psychology in hopes of working with children or the blind, had to have one eye removed when she was six. She has limited vision in her other eye and reads Braille. She explained her decision to accept the lower settlement as follows: "Because of the problems with decisions against handicapped people, I was afraid I'd lose everything. I think I made a wise decision. Everybody said, 'You've got it won!' But I wasn't sure. The others said if I did win they would have appealed the jury decision and there's a chance I would have lost it all. I've been unlucky my whole life. I was just afraid I would be unlucky again." When people asked her how she felt about passing up the $900,000, she replied, "It's a lot of money, but I'm thankful for what I got. It's enough."

Step back a moment and try to analyze the decision this young woman made. She had two immediate alternatives from which to choose: accept the settlement for $165,000, or wait for the verdict, which would promise her much more money if it was in her favor. Once the settlement of $165,000 was offered to her, the outcome of that alternative was certain. If she had decided on the other alternative, she had a good chance of winning, but the judgment would most likely have been appealed, in which case she might have received all of the original amount, a lesser amount, or nothing.

Considering both alternatives, the young woman coupled the known probabilities with some personal probabilities. She thought she was unlucky and therefore found the amount guaranteed by the settlement more attractive. In addition, she said a few things about the desirability of the outcomes for each alternative. The $900,000 possibility appeared more desirable but not so desirable that it was worth turning down a guaranteed amount, although that amount was far less.

As you examine this case, what do you think were the overriding values the young woman brought to her decision? What information was most important to her? What would you have done in this situation? Why?

As you can see, this case is a good example of what is involved in making a choice. A choice is based on your values, goals, information, the risks involved, coupled with the desirability of each possible outcome of your choice. This desirability reflects your values and your goals. Before you make a choice, you develop a plan—consciously or unconsciously—that involves all of these elements in the process. This plan is your personal decisional formula, a kind of strategy for deciding.

Knowing Your Formula for Deciding

It is likely that your decisional formula will vary from choice to choice, although some people do apply the same formula in each critical situation they face. The formula will also differ from person to person, depending on the weight that is attached to each element. People who like to play it safe will put most of the weight on the probabilities involved in the choice. Their attention will focus largely on the likelihood of something happening, and they will tend to choose what is most likely. If you apply this formula to your choices, you will normally trade off desirability for the higher probability of something occurring.

In the malpractice case cited above, it might be said that the young woman was playing it safe, and thus was willing to give up a much larger sum of money. Other people tend to pay more attention to what is desirable and very little attention to the likelihood of its happening. In some decisions, you might identify something that you want so much, something so overpoweringly desirable, that you are not concerned with the probabilities involved. Most of us have a decision plan that is somewhere between the two, although in critical decision situations most people lean toward the play-it-safe side.

What kind of decisional formula do you apply to your critical choices? Put yourself into the malpractice case for a moment. Which option would you choose, the safe one or the high-risk one? Why?

Now, if you rated the greatest risk you've ever taken, would it be on the safe side or the high-risk side? Would it differ from the risk you were willing to take in the above case? Why?

To get the full meaning from your decisional formula, however, we need to look more carefully at desirability. At the lowest level, you can simply rate the desirability of a perceived outcome as good or bad, but after that the real work begins. Turning away from the probabilities involved in the above case, look only at the desirability involved in each of several possible outcomes. Let's say there are four possible outcomes:

Being awarded $900,000
Being awarded a compromise settlement (after an appeal) for $400,000
Accepting the $165,000 settlement
Being awarded nothing after the appeal

Now *rank* these outcomes from 1 (most desirable) to 4 without any other consideration except the desirability of the amount you might win. Your ranking obviously should follow the order listed above. Ranking each in terms of desirability is the second step in evaluating outcomes.

The final step is to determine the comparative differences in desirability between each possible outcome. In the case above, this is relatively simple because the outcomes appear in tangible dollar amounts. Getting to the point where you can determine the comparative desirability of possible outcomes is the highest level you can reach in assessing outcomes. It is a level you should strive for in completing your decisional formula, but it is difficult to attain when the outcomes are less clearly defined than they are here. And this is often so when outcomes relate to qualities such as integrity, success, prestige, and satisfaction—rather than to sums of money.

Even such intangible outcomes, however, can be evaluated and compared. In some business situations, they are even quantified. Some years ago, a management study indicated that one subsidiary of a company was losing four million dollars a year. When questioned about this loss, corporate decision-makers said that this subsidiary returned other dividends, such as good will in the community and a good image for the corporation as a whole, and that it contributed to the profits being made in other divisions. Initially, they said that they could not place a dollar value on these qualities, but when pressed, they admitted they would not be willing to allow the subsidiary to lose as much as ten million dollars a year. Ultimately, they were able to place a dollar amount on the "worth" of a good image, good will in the community, and an intangible contribution to profits. So, in addition to making a more accurate assessment of how desirable something was, they were also beginning to establish how much they were willing to "pay" to maintain that outcome (more on this "cost" factor later).

Now let's look again at the executive caught in the conflict of getting to the top. If he works longer hours, he will have more resources with which to care for his family, but less time to spend with them. In this case, he must make every effort to spell out what each value is worth. Can he amass more pay and prestige if he gives up only one family weekend a month? Two? Where will he draw the line? When all of the elements are assessed individually and then compared in terms of their value to the decider, he can begin to rate one over the other and then begin to determine the differences between each in terms of its desirability.

Here is another case full of intangibles. Pat is a thirty-year-old promotional and marketing expert who has a good job with a promising future in a solid company. Recently, however, Pat has become increasingly interested in being involved in management, and such opportunities are limited in her present company. She decides to apply for an innovative M.B.A. program for young executives that is being offered by one of the most prestigious business schools in the country. Much to her surprise, she is accepted into the program. The program is for twenty weeks, and all classes meet on the weekends except for one day each month when students meet in a special seminar. While Pat's immediate supervisor approves her request to take off one day a month to pursue the M.B.A. program, she is told by *his* superior that she cannot do it— even if she decides to take vacation time to cover her absence from the office.

Pat's first impulse is to quit and find another job, but several factors make her hesitate. Currently she is support-ing her unemployed husband and their seven-year-old daughter. She wonders what her being without a job for even a short period of time would do to her family.

Besides, she is reluctant to give up her job, which, on the whole, is excellent. Her boss has also told her that she'll never find anything better in the present job market. What if she cannot get another job at all? However, when Pat assesses what she wants, she finds that the M.B.A. and the advantages of that degree are more important than anything else. She also knows that she may not get another chance to get into a program that fits her needs so well.

Pat is at a critical decision point. She knows what she wants, but she is not sure about the risk she is willing to take to get it. She realizes that whatever alternative she chooses will carry some risk for her, for her future, and for her family. She also knows she has to work out her alternatives, predict their outcomes, and compare them on the basis of probability and desirability. Then she will be in a better position to decide if the risks are worth it to her in terms of her values and goals.

To get started, Pat listed each alternative and tried to predict the possible outcomes.

Alternatives Under Consideration

1. Quit job and pursue M.B.A.
2. Stay with job, forget M.B.A. for now.

Outcomes in Terms of Probability and Desirability for

Alternative #1	*Alternative #2*
Loss of income (not certain about getting another job; not desirable to be without income for even a short period of time).	Uninterrupted support for family (certainty).
Possible deterioration of family relationships (no problem as long as have job; undesirable to have existing good relationships deteriorate).	Family relations continue as usual (but may feel resentment regarding self-satisfaction; undesirable).
	Poor attitude toward job (very probable; very undesirable).

Get M.B.A. (very probable and most desirable outcome).

Loss of an opportunity that may not present itself again (highly likely and very undesirable in terms of future and self-satisfaction).

Pat did assume that she could get another job, but she was not sure how soon, or even if she could get time off in a new job situation. To develop greater certainty about these possibilities, she decided to talk to people from other companies, as she needed better information about current job opportunities. Her family security would not be jeopardized if she got another job soon. On the other hand, she wondered what the additional pressure of her being unemployed would actually do to her relationship with her husband. Still, if she did quit, she could get her M.B.A., which she noted as having the highest desirability for her.

Staying on the job and forgoing the M.B.A. was desirable only in terms of the family financial picture. The greatest risk relating to security and family relations stemmed from quitting her job, which seemed the most desirable alternative by far in terms of what she wanted.

Much to her surprise and delight, Pat's information-seeking about other jobs quickly pointed up two things. First, that there were other opportunities in her field; and second, that most companies were encouraging employees to pursue career-development programs. In other words, Pat found it was highly probable that she could get another position and still pursue the M.B.A. She submitted her letter of resignation and within a week received several job offers. In addition, she unexpectedly received higher salary offers as well. By going through the decision-making process, she made a good decision for herself, her future, and her family.

Your Critical Decision

This step involves pulling things together. On the chart on the next page, fill in the alternatives along with the outcomes you see as possible for each. Then attach a probability value to each of those outcomes. If you know what the probability is (for example, salary of $35,000 per year), put it down; or you may simply indicate what the chances appear to be for that outcome. Remember, I'm assuming that you have done your work and collected good information to help you determine the probabilities involved. If you do not have good information or cannot get it, take an educated guess at the probabilities, but keep in mind that you may want to gather more information in the future.

YOUR CRITICAL DECISION

Alternatives	Possible Outcomes	Probability for Each Outcome	Desirability of Outcomes		
	(Include anything that might result if you choose the alternative.)	(If you know the probability, put it down. If not, put down better than 75% likelihood; 50–75% likelihood; 20–50% likelihood; 1–25% likelihood.)	Good or Bad	Rank "1" for most desirable outcome and continue to rank all the way down to the least desirable.	Comparative difference (Look at the ranked outcomes and attach a value of from 1 to 10 [highest value] to each outcome. No two different outcomes should have the same value.)

Now develop your decisional formula by making a statement weighing probability and desirability as they relate to each alternative.

What Alternative Do You Select? Why?

9.

Taking Action

To decide is useless if the decision cannot
be carried out.
—John Galsworthy, *Flowering Wilderness*

Now that you've gone through all the phases of the
decision-making process, you should be ready to make a
commitment and actually put your choice into action. As
you prepare, a lot of last-minute thoughts may be running
through your mind. These are potential obstacles that
could prevent you from getting what you want. "I want
to take action now," you might say to yourself, "but what
about family responsibilities? This wavering, anxious
feeling I have? The way others feel? Money? The uncertainty that it will work out? My lack of complete
confidence? Time? The possibility of failing in some way?
The unexpected consequences? What I'm going to have
to give up?"

If one or more of these apply to you and your critical
decision, circle the items and ask yourself some of the
following clarifying questions.

In what way will my decision enhance my life? Do I
value the opportunity for a better life enough to deal with
the action obstacles that may prevent me from getting
what I want and need?

What kind of changes will I have to make in my life to
achieve greater satisfaction? How will any of the action
obstacles affect those changes?

How will significant people in my life know that I'm

taking action? What will I have to do to prepare them for the action I am about to take?

Finally, and perhaps most important, what can I do to prevent myself or others from sabotaging my efforts to take action? Of the action obstacles above, which might give me a clue to a possible area of sabotage?

Things That Might Prevent Me from Putting My Decision Into Action

_____

_____

_____

_____

_____

_____

How I Might Sabotage Myself	How Others Might Sabotage My Efforts
Example:	
By not giving it enough time	By asking for more of my time
_____	_____
_____	_____
_____	_____
_____	_____

Remember that just by taking action you'll be out ahead of the pack, and by taking action after making a well-considered choice you're apt to be way ahead. But when you begin to move out, you may also miss the kind of reinforcement that you were getting in the pack. You will find very quickly that you are going to be questioned more about your actions. Consequently, you'll be forced to take a more careful look at what you are up to.

Even if you're making a "conforming" critical choice such as marriage, if you stick up for your decision in a confident way because you've considered it well, it will help you to keep moving toward what you want in life. And it is at this initial challenge to defend their acts that many people back off, because they lack confidence. Self-doubt becomes their prison, the major factor in limiting their life potential.

One thing that will help you if you have to defend your decision is the ability to bring a thorough and accurate assessment of your strengths to your critical decision point. Even more important is to be on solid ground regarding how you went about making the decision that you are about to act upon. As far as your decision is concerned, you are the one and only expert. You have to believe that you are authentic in your role as decision-maker, and you have to communicate this to others.

Becoming Authentic as a Decision-Maker

By "authentic," I mean that you have developed your decision-making skills and can convince others, if necessary, that you have applied them correctly. You have related each step in the decision-making process to your own situation—in terms of what is important to you, what you want, and what you are willing to risk for what you want. Once you have done this, nobody else—your doctor, psychiatrist, spouse, or mother-in-law—can be a substitute authentic decision-maker for you. Your authenticity is what is uniquely yours in a given situation. Good advice is nice, but, like experience, it should be treated as information, and the greatest expert can only give you advice about your decisions.

If this is difficult to imagine, try to put yourself in the following situation. You have at your disposal an expert on retirement who has more information about retirement possibilities than anyone else in the world. He also knows you as well as your closest friend does. He offers his services to make decisions about your retirement. You may discuss with him or even submit in writing your goals and values and the amount of money you have to commit to your retirement plans. The one stipulation is that once you accept his offer you must abide by his decision. How would you feel about this person making this important choice for you? What does this expert lack in terms of authenticity? Why might you be more comfortable making this decision yourself? Can you really be more authentic than this expert? Of course you can. You are more authentic because you are the best authority about yourself —or at least you have the potential for being the best authority.

But in building your authenticity, you'll have to go beyond merely knowing what the decision-making process is and how it can be applied to your life. You must also have a good sense of the freedom you have for making choices. As a decider, you have certain rights that at times will be denied you by others. Remember that whatever the neighbors, your parents, or your boss may say, you are *free* to decide things such as to quit work, to choose not to work in a productive fashion, to insist that your children foot the bill for college, or to return to work shortly after giving birth to a child. In your drive to be authentic in your decision-making, it will be crucial to get a good grasp of your freedoms in order to deal with the people (including yourself) and institutions who will deny —sometimes subtly and sometimes quite openly and aggressively—your right to decide for yourself.

Take a look now at your own *authenticity profile:*

Do you feel okay about making decisions but not about carrying them out?	Yes	No
Do you sometimes give up the choice you want without standing up for it?	Yes	No
Are you reluctant to tell somebody how you feel about something, even when it's important to you?	Yes	No

Do you hesitate to voice your own opinion when you're in the minority?	Yes	No
Do you feel unsure about your rights as a decider?	Yes	No
Have you let others make important decisions that you have had to live with?	Yes	No

If most of your answers were yes, you may need to build up a higher degree of confidence in your right to carry out your decisions. The following real-life example should steer your thinking about this in the right direction.

Recently, in my town there was a proposal by a group of parents to initiate a lunch program in their elementary schools. The program was to be entirely funded and organized by parents who wanted to take part for a variety of reasons: relief for working mothers, an option for parents who could not always get home at lunchtime, a way to accommodate parents who had children in different schools or who could not afford to get help during the lunch hours.

Soon an aggressive counterattack was launched by other parents to defeat this proposal. Among their reasons were: that children benefit from having lunch at home; and that if both parents in a family had to work, thus neglecting their children, then perhaps they shouldn't live in this particular town. The opposition group seemed to be saying that there was no choice in the matter. Many parents who supported the lunch program made the same interpretation and withdrew their support because they believed there was no choice. Remember, this program was to apply only to those parents who wanted it. It was never intended for the entire district, school, or even one class in one school.

While the pro-lunch-plan parents could articulate why they supported the program, they were not authentic when it came to defending their freedom to choose as individuals. Knowing your rights and freedoms as a decision-maker may make a real difference in carrying out the action you want to take.

A Decider's Bill of Rights

Apart from any legal or religious constraints that you feel you must observe (and you can even decide to act illegally or sacrilegiously), you are technically free to decide anything having to do with your life. You are even free to fail, to die, and to work without monetary reward. You also have:

- The right to decide something for yourself even if there is nobody else who thinks you should decide that way.
- The right to express your feelings to others in the context of explaining your choice.
- The right to say "no" without feeling guilty.
- The right to decide about the use of and the way you commit your resources, including your time.
- The right to ask others to consider you when they make a choice or when they question your choice.
- The right not to have all the answers.
- The right to use emotions in the decisions you make.
- The right to share your opinion with the expectation that others will listen.
- The right to admit you made a poor decision, to do something about it, and to continue to make more decisions.
- The right to do what is important to you, including being nice to yourself.

Knowing these rights and freedoms not only helps you take action and stick up for your decision, but it also gives you a sound basis for the assertive behavior you may have to demonstrate in order to get what you want. Assertiveness, as used here, is simply standing up for your own rights without rejecting another person or violating his rights. In knowing your rights, you'll feel more authentic in the pursuit of your goals. You will also be more alert to any attempt to take away those rights.

Consequently, when somebody tells me that a lunch program is harmful and that I should vote against it, I don't need to say "I guess you're right" because I don't think I have a right to my feelings. I don't need to say "Why don't you think more than talk and perhaps you'd see the need for a lunch program," because then I would be denying the right of that person to a differing opinion. I *can* say, quite assertively, "I understand your feelings, but working parents such as myself need options like this if we're to insure the best possible care for our children. Isn't that what you're concerned about?" Or, to put it another way, "I can see your point and I'd like to be able to tend to my children at lunchtime. But in my circumstances I can't. I'd be glad to explain why this is the best option for me and my children."

Consider the following situations and assume that you have gone through the decision-making process carefully for each. How would you respond authentically if:

You decide to quit your job and take a year off touring the country in a camper with your wife and two children, and your parents tell you that you are jeopardizing your future and your family's?

_____

_____

You decide on divorce to resolve a deteriorating relationship that you feel you cannot stand any more, and your spouse, your parents, and your in-laws say you can't get a divorce because of the children?

_____

_____

You are very happy with your job and are doing well, but you decide to retire early so you will be able to do some of the things you've always wanted to do, and your associates tell you you're foolish, that people are not generally happy when they retire early?

_____

_____

After fifteen years of work in one profession, you decide at age forty-five to return to school to prepare for a very different occupation, and all the people around you say that this is an admirable idea but that it is too late for you—you can't change careers at this point in your life?

_____

_____

In your responses, have you indicated how you prepared yourself for making the choice—that is, the aspects of the situation you considered in the decision-making process? Have you effectively expressed the rights and explained the freedom you have as the decider in each case?

Planning Ahead for the Consequences of Your Decisions

A final element of authentic decision-making is planning or looking ahead. Too often, people tend to manage the crisis or decision point at hand without looking ahead to some of the long-range consequences of the present crisis. You lose some of your authenticity when you cannot respond to the question "What are you going to do after that year of touring around and thinking in your camper?" While it is not necessary to have a specific answer in mind, it is important to have a sense of direction.

Being authentic, then, may require that you have at least a credible long-range plan thought through for yourself. It is a lot easier to feel authentic and to convey that authenticity if you are able to discuss how you might handle some of the consequences of your choice. Remember that one decision leads to others. Planning ahead will give you a better chance to control the rest of your life effectively. It might help you to try to develop a series of responses to the inevitable "What if?" questions.

What Would Happen If

You didn't find any answers in your year away from work?

_____

Your divorce had some negative impact on the children?

_____

You found that you didn't like retirement?

_____

Your move to a new career had severe financial hardship associated with it?

_____

Your Critical Decision

Try to think of some "What if?" questions you might have to answer if you decided to act on the alternative you chose.

The Alternative You Chose: _____

"What would happen if" questions you might have to answer:	Your responses to those questions:
_____	_____
_____	_____
_____	_____
_____	_____

The Time for Action

In the final analysis, being authentic as a decision-maker is knowing why you're deciding a certain way and deciding with the full realization of your rights as an individual. It is being able to articulate what you're going to do to control your life and why you're doing it. And it is assuming responsibility for the consequences of the action you take. The commitment to act, to actually get moving, will be accelerated if you feel genuine about your planned action and if you can communicate this authenticity as a decision-maker.

Many people think the only time for action in their lives is in emergency situations. The inference is that the task in decision-making is merely to get rid of a crisis and go on to something else. In fact, you will find as you become aware of your choices and begin to plan for action that the critical decision point represents a really positive opportunity to add assets and strengths to your life. The skilled decision-maker treats his decision point as a time for opportunity and growth, while the person who shrinks from choice sees it at best as a time to neutralize crisis so that nothing worse happens.

Several years ago in Seattle, large numbers of highly paid engineers lost their jobs because of the decreased demand for their services in a previously booming industry. For most of these people, the loss of highly paid positions on very short notice created a point of crisis in their lives. Their responses to this crisis varied widely. Some of the engineers continued to look for related work in the very same area, where there was now a surfeit of unemployed engineers. This group tended to treat the crisis as something to get rid of by simply finding new employment as quickly as possible in the kind of job they most preferred or thought they were most qualified for. They neglected the elements of the decision-making setting in which they were operating and did little to formulate goals and develop new alternatives for themselves—given the fact that the probability of being employed as an engineer had been reduced practically to zero. Others, facing the same crisis, decided on different alternatives, which included upgrading their skills in other areas of engineering or doing something else they had always wanted to do, in most cases unrelated to engineering.

For all these people, losing their work so suddenly created a crisis that carried with it a number of hardships. But those who were able to develop alternatives, to refashion their goals and take a clear look at the setting in which they were operating, were often able to deal with the crisis and convert it into a unique and satisfying opportunity in their lives. In other words, they treated the situation as something they could deal with and gain control over. They took a stand at the start that permitted them to move forward, as opposed to taking whatever was offered them by circumstances. Some, who waited for something to happen, did so in vain because nothing came along. In effect, they were choosing not to decide. As a result, they considerably reduced their chances of getting what they wanted.

Opportunity in a critical situation is created by the decider who is not content with the prospect of letting the chips fall where they may.

The Cost of Action—Is It Worth It?

Regardless of which path you do choose, there is a cost involved. That is the fear that engulfs many people as they implement a choice. To act means to do, to give, and to commit at least some of your resources. It is a transaction in which you are willing to give something in order to get something in return. You must relinquish some of your precious resources in order to get something that is important to you. The goal that makes you give up something worthwhile can be your opportunity of a lifetime— but you'll only get it by taking action.

There are several things to consider if you are hesitating over the cost of your decision. First, when you take action you may seem to be all alone, because you are going from the known and comfortable to something less known and less comfortable. Yet your action puts you in contact with other possibilities that never would have occurred if you stayed where you were. So while you may have to give up something to take action, you may be gaining not only an immediate result but also a chance to do many more things in the future.

Second, the move to act may not yield the success you

anticipated. Perhaps that new job doesn't turn out to be what you expected. Even if you experience a kind of nonsuccess with some of your actions, you do not necessarily fail. The fact that you were able to decide, to act, is a learning process in itself, which is likely to pay dividends at future critical decision points in your life. If, for example, early retirement does not turn out to be what you expected or hoped for, you have nonetheless learned something about yourself that may contribute to the quality of the rest of your life. With each decision you make, you'll find subsequent decisions easier for you, especially if you examine the process of each choice, even those that do not turn out to your liking.

Third, although you may worry about the cost in *time* involved, it is rarely too late to take action. By late, I'm talking about attaching some arbitrary age limitation to your decisions. Typically, middle-aged persons hesitate to start new careers because they fear that, after the retraining period, they will have only a few years to work in their new field. And so they may spend those same years dissatisfied with a job that no longer interests them! You should consider the worth of the action in terms of the *quality* it may give to your life—even if it is for a short period of time.

Recently, a man told me that the best year of his life— the happiest and most worthwhile—was the one when he served as a house parent for a group of delinquent boys. Many people go through life without anything approaching this kind of high point, often because of the feeling that they do not have the time to reach out for it.

Reaching can be inhibited when what you're reaching for seems unknown and in some respects downright terrifying. Often this comes about because the decider is looking at a vague kind of result that may follow a good action. You have the feeling that you should take action but—? One practical way to help you take the action step in this situation is to try to articulate in specific terms the worst thing that could happen. A person contemplating going into his own business might say, "The worst thing that can result from this action is that I'll lose the capital I invested and I'll have to go back to a full-time job." Or the family considering adoption might say, "A child living with us will disrupt the existing harmonious relations that we have in our family." Once the "worst" result is stated with some specificity, it is much easier to determine whether or not the action is worth what might evolve.

There are some useful guidelines to consider when you assess the worth of the risk you are taking in committing yourself to a new action:

Can you afford this action in terms of time, energy, and other resources?

Is the payoff adequate in terms of the risk you are taking?

Does the action support your goals and values?

What problems will this action create in terms of the people and the world around you?

Are there any predictable changes or uncertainties that might spell disaster if you take this action?

10.
Being Responsive
to Your Choice

The ability to arrive at complex decisions should be the hallmark of the educated person. Indeed, it should be what education, as opposed to instruction or training, is all about.

In this tense, ever more crowded, ever more interdependent world, decision-making is becoming more and more crucial. I do not hesitate to proclaim that the future of the human race will depend on whether our graduates, citizens of the greatest democracy on earth, members of the most highly developed technological society in the world, have the wisdom and the courage to make, and to carry out, the right decisions.

—Dr. Jean Mayer, President of Tufts University

Authentic decision-making does not end when you take action. When you begin to take control of your life by making decisions, you are responsible for the choices you make. Although there is some evidence to the contrary, we do not live in a no-fault society. The contingencies and consequences of your choices should not and cannot be ignored.

If you run for public office and find yourself sacrificing your ideals in order to get more votes, you may rationalize by saying that the end justifies the means. But you should also be aware that there is a cost factor involved in giving up those ideals for more votes. The same is true in any field. The president of a large bank recently told me in an interview, "It's much easier to get your values across when you are on top than it is when you're on the way up." True, but I would add: Don't forget the cost of forgoing your values on the way to the top. That cost may affect what you can do about those values when you reach the top.

Even if you have simply done what others have told you to do, you are not totally free of responsibility. Your superiors or other important people in your life may have the ultimate responsibility, but your act will also elicit some cost from you. The political revelations of the 1970s have given us many examples of this problem of ultimate responsibility. The Watergate scandals, the disclosures relating to the widespread practice of bribery for favor in industry, and the illegal invasion of privacy sanctioned by intelligence-gathering agencies all involved orders from the top. However, many of the underlings who took action based on these orders were held accountable, and their lives were permanently affected as a result of their actions. So keep in mind that even if you act on someone else's decision, you are liable to be held accountable in part or in full for what you do.

Another aspect of responsiveness is reassessing the decision you have acted on and making timely corrections before your mistakes, if any, are compounded. If you recognize that you have made a poor decision, do something about it! Admit that you made a mistake and search for another action that will remedy the error. At least do not continue to pour valuable resources into a poor decision.

One of the best examples of not doing anything to correct a bad decision was evidenced in the Vietnam War. Very early in the conflict, years before any corrective action was taken, a number of government leaders recognized that the decision-making process involved from the very beginning was weak, to say the least. However, so much was committed to solving this problem militarily that resources continued to be poured into Vietnam, even after the war was recognized as a mistake by the military, the State Department, the Congress, and the executive branch. Troop build-up continued in spite of the information that the increase was not bringing the war to a speedy end. As Peter Bourne, Washington psychiatrist on the Walter Reed research team in Vietnam during 1966, indicated, "The overwhelming desire for the success of policies to which a strong emotional attachment has been made also leads to an attempt to alter those facts over which one has control, making them consistent with the outcome that is desired. It is as though there is an expectation at a magical level that events over which one has no control will fall into the desired pattern."

The behavior of these decision-makers is an example of a situation in which you let a poor decision force you into an untenable position. First you try to make the decision work. When this doesn't get you anywhere, you begin to justify the choice as being the best available. While it isn't a glowing success, you say, it is better than the other choices would be. Sometimes this declaration is quite sincere. Generally, however, it is not true. At the stage of trying to force the decision, a lot of things are happening—including something called "cognitive dissonance."

Cognitive dissonance takes place when you consciously or unconsciously begin to screen out information and opinions that might call your choice into question. You begin to look for only that information which will support your point of view and listen to only those who agree with you. This is mainly because you have committed so much to the decision that you feel by now you can't afford to be wrong. And so we shut out the input we need to reassess our choice and make a better one another time.

While your action is a kind of culminating point in each decision you make, the decision does not end with the action itself. In a sense it never ends, because you are always assessing the action in terms of new changes, uncertainties, and information about yourself and your decision-making setting. A leading car salesman remarked some time ago that when you move a car owner from a big to a small car you rarely put a smile on that person's face, but when you move the small-car owner to a big car you have a much better chance of getting a smile. This is not to say that it is good or bad to buy a small car or a big car. The real moral of the story is "What in the end will make me smile about my decision? If I'm still grimacing about it after I've taken action, perhaps it is important to reassess my choice." Life is a precious commodity. You have a relatively short period of time to get what you want. By reassessing your choices honestly and carefully, you can begin to reduce wasted time—or the time it takes to get back on the track of what you want after making a wrong turn in your life journey.

Now, the idea of being responsive to a choice should not be confused with what might be described as "backward think," a kind of regressive process. Backward think occurs when you take action and then ruefully and regretfully begin to turn your attention to what you have given up in taking it. If the result does not immediately turn out to be what was expected, some people make a quick scramble to recapture what they have given up before they give the alternative they have chosen a chance to work out. The catch phrase of this situation is, "If only I had . . ." If you're not careful, you end up thinking only of your mistakes and lose any chance you have of moving forward by correcting and making the best of your choice. Typically, when you do look back, you begin to think that other alternatives you gave up look better. However, most people get into this situation because they have done a poor job of selecting the best alternative in the first place. Looking back can be a useful exercise in assessing how wisely you decided, but it should not interfere with your movement toward what you want in life. Rather, it is a good chance to incorporate the things you overlooked into the *next* goal you formulate and into the *next* act you commit. Being responsive means using in your future choices whatever hindsight you have developed in your past ones.

Your Critical Decision

Let's look back now at your critical decision:

Something I Gave Up to Make My Critical Decision _____

_____

Why I Regret Giving This Up _____

_____

When you have done this, consider a new goal that will help you recapture at least part of what you gave up.

A New Goal _____

_____

What are the major mistakes you want to correct? What values do you want to include in this new goal statement?

Mistakes Recognized from a Previous Action and Values I Want to Consider _____

_____

With this in mind, develop several alternatives that will help you reach your new goal. Explain how these courses of action will not include the mistakes you made in your last choice.

Courses of Action (Alternatives)	How Previous Mistakes and Other Considerations Have Been Remedied
_____	_____
_____	_____

You can carry this out by gathering new information, assessing the probability and desirability of the outcomes of each alternative you are now considering, and employing your decisional formula to make a new decision. Does this decision get you what you want, or closer to some ultimate goal you have?

Life Is Full of Choices

And so you see that decision-making never ends. The more decisions you make, the more life choices you will become conscious of, and the more space and freedom you will be claiming for yourself. As you confront your life full of choices, keep these guidelines in mind:

1. *Don't Undersell Yourself.* Develop a careful personal résumé for yourself. Remember what you do well, and the experiences you've had—even if those experiences aren't the kind that would typically fit into a job application or a college admissions form. Then tell people about yourself and about those things that qualify you for getting what you want.

2. *Take Small Action Steps First.* You need not take the leap from your starting point to your ultimate goal all at once. There are usually some intermediate steps that will get you started and keep you moving toward that goal. For instance, if you want to develop a career after years at home, related volunteer work, part-time study, or more

intensive commitment to a hobby might be the first and best action steps for you to take.

3. *Be the Kind of Person on Whom Nothing Is Lost.* Observe, read, experience, and explore everything in the context of some goal you have set. Constantly add dimensions to your experience that will help you achieve the long-range goal you have in mind for yourself.

4. *Think Ahead.* Anticipate what might happen if you are stalled on the way to your goal or if the action you take does not live up to your expectations. Have a few "What will I do if?" questions in mind as you take even the first action steps.

5. *Learn from Action.* Keep evaluating the meaning and results of your actions and revising your ultimate goal accordingly. Even if your action does not turn out satisfactorily, you can learn from it.

6. *Revise Your Personal Résumé Frequently.* As you take action, and as you constantly learn more about yourself, update your personal résumé to include new skills and resources. Do this by keeping a personal log of growth experiences, things you've learned about yourself and things you've done.

7. *Remember That Few Decisions Are Irreversible.* Most of the time you'll have at least a second chance. It is true that with each decision you give up something, but you also tend to gain new knowledge that can be plugged into a new decision that will help you realize more satisfying outcomes.

8. *Don't Sit on Your Action.* It's great to feel good about an action you've taken, but when you have acted, think about what you're going to do next. Keep up your momentum!

9. *Don't Get Hung Up on Results.* Even a good decision can yield poor results, and the best decision-makers can come up with very unsatisfactory outcomes. Instead

of wasting your time on regret, try to determine what went wrong in your choice. Think about how you made the decision, how you applied the decision-making process, so the results will be better the next time.

10. *Your Decision Is a Definition of Yourself.* Try to be more than what you are at the moment. Try hard to set the ceiling you want on life and know that your expectations for yourself need to be clarified before any direction is possible.

Above all, remember that in most cases some action will be better than no action at all. To put it another way, making no decision at all is often far more destructive than making a poor decision. When you follow a no-decision pattern in life, you are defaulting the chance to have the kind of life you want. The absence of a decision means you have not subjected your current course of action to scrutiny. Your current course of action may be the best one for you, but at least make it a conscious choice. To give up the opportunity to define yourself is to give up your freedom to decide what you want to become. And as you go past the midpoint of your life, the sum of your results so far may not be impressive, especially not to the person who counts the most—you!

Oliver Wendell Holmes put it best when he said, "Life is painting a picture, not doing a sum." The action you take in life is what will ultimately paint your picture. You're the one critic who will be faced with the task of judging the work you have created.